Outdoor Emergency Medicine

Outdoor Emergency Medicine

Frank C. Madda, M.D., Editor

Contemporary Books, Inc.
Chicago

Mention of proprietary products in this book does not constitute an endorsement of the products. They are included because of their easy access and familiarity to most persons.

Published by Contemporary Books, Inc.
180 North Michigan Avenue, Chicago, Illinois 60601
Manufactured in the United States of America
Library of Congress Catalog Card Number: 81-71082
International Standard Book Number: 0-8092-5774-2 (cloth)
                                    0-8092-5773-4 (paper)

Published simultaneously in Canada by
Beaverbooks, Ltd.
150 Lesmill Road
Don Mills, Ontario M3B 2T5
Canada

To my wife Debbie, whose encouragement
and understanding made this book
possible.

About the Editor

THE EDITOR and main contributing author of this book is Frank C. Madda, B.S., D.D.S., M.D., M.S., with training in Oral Surgery, General Surgery, and Plastic and Reconstructive Surgery at Rush-Presbyterian-St. Luke's Medical Center, and is now in private practice at Good Samaritan Hospital in Downers Grove, Illinois. His two loves are medicine and the outdoors, and this book is a marriage of those two loves.

Preface

I have hunted, fished, and camped from Hudson Bay to the Florida Keys, from Ohio to Montana. Being a dentist, a physician, and an avid outdoorsman, I have seen and been called on to help in many backcountry emergencies. I have also seen that many people who enjoy the outdoors lack practical medical knowledge.

There are a great many books for the outdoorsman. The shelves are filled with how to tie flies, how to recognize and identify game, how to track, and how to cook. While all of these things are interesting and useful, and add to our enjoyment of the outdoors and our sporting activities, frequently we all overlook the most important piece of equipment we have—our own bodies. We service and polish our equipment until it gleams but spend relatively little time preparing our bodies for the out-of-doors.

For those of us who find our greatest moments of pleasure many miles from medical aid, I have never seen a book that definitively told people how to care for themselves or others until they can get to a doctor, or how to recognize which problems need medical attention. I think this book can give the sportsman and his family a working knowledge of what to do without trying to make doctors of them. It is not the intention of this book that its information should be used instead of seeking medical aid. The purpose of this book is to provide the correct things to do until emergency medical attention can be reached. All advice is documented as the presently accepted medical emergency care—both by the medical literature and by specialists in each field discussed.

This book does not just tell you to be careful outdoors—as an outdoorsman, you should know that already. This book will tell you the right things to do when the unexpected happens outdoors—in spite of your being careful.

So go out into the mountains, the forests, and the streams; enjoy the out-of-doors fully. With the information that you will obtain from reading this book, I know that you will have a new sense of confidence in knowing that whatever situations can arise you will be prepared to deal with them in the best possible way. It will also make you feel good knowing that after you have taken care of all the rest of your equipment that the one irreplaceable piece that you have—yourself—can also be properly taken care of should the necessity arise. After all, most outdoorsmen want to feel totally independent and on their own when they are out in the wilderness. I hope that this book will add to that feeling of having the ability to handle every situation which arises and add to the overall enjoyment of the outdoors for you.

TABLE OF CONTENTS

LIST OF CONTRIBUTORS

The editor of this book is indebted to a number of professional associates and friends who have contributed their time and effort to the publication of this book. Specifically,

Ruth S. Campanella, M.D., Rush-Presbyterian-St. Luke's Medical Center, Chicago, Illinois
Emergencies Involving the Ear

Robert Chesney, M.D., F.R.C.S., Aberdeen, Scotland
Injuries to the Arm and Hand

Charles M. D'Angelo, M.D., Rush-Presbyterian-St. Luke's Medical Center, Chicago, Illinois
Head and Spinal Cord Injuries

Dino S. Delicata, M.D., Good Samaritan Hospital, Downers Grove, Illinois
When the Problem Is the Airway

Alexander Doolas, M.D., Rush-Presbyterian-St. Luke's Medical Center, Chicago, Illinois
Chest and Abdominal Injuries

Bruce Greenspahn, M.D., The University of Chicago Hospitals and Clinics, Chicago, Illinois
The Sportsman at High Altitudes

Michael F. Haklin, Rush-Presbyterian-St. Luke's Medical Center, Chicago, Illinois
Cardiopulmonary Resuscitation

John M. Jones, M.D., F.R.C.S., Wales, Great Britain
Leg Injuries

Allan Luskin, M.D., Rush-Presbyterian-St. Luke's Medical Center, Chicago, Illinois
Stinging Insect Reactions

Frank C. Madda, M.D., Good Samaritan Hospital, Downers Grove, Illinois
General Health in the Outdoors, Burns, Poisoning from Spiders, Snakes, and Coelenterates, Problems in the Cold, Problems with the Sun and Heat, The Emergency Kit, Selected Poison Control Centers

Ronald L. Meng, M.D., Rush-Presbyterian-St. Luke's Medical Center, Chicago, Illinois
The Solo Wilderness Traveler

R. J. Olk, M.D., Washington University, St. Louis, Missouri
Emergency Eye Problems in the Outdoors

Robert Passavoy, M.D., Rush-Presbyterian-St. Luke's Medical Center, Chicago, Illinois
Nutrition and Water Balance

Mark Rosenberg, M.D., Sherman Hospital, Elgin, Illinois
Sharing the Outdoors with Children

Mark J. Round, M.D., Chicago, Illinois
The Sportsperson and Chronic Disease

Z. L. G. Stein, R.Ph., Rush-Presbyterian-St. Luke's Poison Control Center, Chicago, Illinois
Poisoning from Dangerous Plants

Thomas G. Suttie, R.Ph., Rush-Presbyterian-St. Luke's Poison Control Center, Chicago, Illinois
Chemical and Food Poisoning in the Outdoors

Gary M. Trager, M.D., University of Illinois College of Medicine, Chicago, Illinois
The Outdoorsperson and Infectious Disease

Richard J. Wren, D.D.S., Chicago, Illinois
Dental Problems Outdoors

Special thanks to two very talented individuals for their excellent illustrations. Namely,

Cheryl Haugh, Rush-Presbyterian-St. Luke's Medical Center, Chicago, Illinois
Medical Illustrator

Michael Carroll, Rush-Presbyterian-St. Luke's Medical Center, Chicago, Illinois
Medical Illustrator

Also, for copyediting, Veronica Gaber, BioService Corporation, and all those too numerous to name who provided support and assistance.

Frank C. Madda, M.D., June, 1980

1

General Health in the Outdoors

I would like to welcome you to a new book in which we will explore being healthy and staying healthy in the outdoors. There is no single group of people who need to know more about taking care of themselves than those of us who venture out into the forests, mountains, and water ways in pursuit of our favorite pastimes—hunting, fishing, and camping. Frequently our wanderings take us into areas where medical assistance is either several hours away or nearly impossible to reach. This book will give you the basic information you need to avoid many problems, recognize the early symptoms of a problem developing, and provide a plan of action for you to engage in to prevent a major problem from developing. It will be commonsense talk about all too common problems.

Honesty is the best preventive medicine. You may have been the toughest kid in your gym class in 1958, but what kind of shape are you in *right now?* Be honest! The work many of us do for most of the year does not give us the physical challenges that keep strength and stamina at peak performance. This is where honesty comes into play. Try to evaluate your present state of fitness critically. Take into consideration any special health problems you may have, such as diabetes, asthma, a history of heart attack, etc. Then lay down some sensible limits for yourself. You wouldn't expect your old 12-gauge to knock down a goose that is 150 yards away—give your body the same consideration.

Frequently I have heard people in hunting and

11

fishing camps saying how great it is to be outdoors and getting into shape again. I think they are missing the point. The trip you have saved for all year is *not* the time or place to get into shape. I have seen too many disappointed faces when someone finds out that they have to hunt or fish near base camp because they are unable physically to get where they want to go. The time to get yourself ready for the trip is long before you depart. We all spend weeks and even months getting our gear into top shape and sighting in our guns before a trip. But how much time do we spend getting ourselves ready? Some of us devote a little time to this phase of the preparation, but most of us give it no time at all. Being winded and having sore arms and legs that won't do what you want them to can spoil any trip. Getting into shape is easy, and this is the first and most important step in staying healthy outdoors. Remember, you are not preparing for the Olympic decathlon, you are preparing to enjoy hunting, fishing, and/or backpacking. So let's lay out our plans with that in mind.

First, walking across a field carrying three shotguns would wear anyone out, and every 8½ pounds you are overweight is like carrying an extra shotgun. If you are overweight, the first step in shaping up is slimming down. You will be amazed at how losing those pounds will increase your exercise tolerance, which is stamina. Ideal body weight varies by height, build (bone size), sex, and age. Take a look at the body weight chart and judge your build, and you will get a good idea of what your weight should be, allowing five pounds either way. Then you can see how many extra "shotguns" you have been carrying around.

Desirable Weights for Men and Women Aged 25 and Over (in pounds according to height and frame, in indoor clothing)

For ages 18-25 subtract 1 lb. for each year under 25 years.

Height		Small Frame	Medium Frame	Large Frame
with 1" heels		**MEN**		
Feet	**Inches**			
5	2	112-120	118-129	126-141
5	3	115-123	121-133	129-144
5	4	118-126	124-136	132-148
5	5	121-129	127-139	135-152
5	6	124-133	130-143	138-156
5	7	128-137	134-147	142-161
5	8	132-141	138-152	147-166
5	9	136-145	142-156	151-170
5	10	140-150	146-160	155-174
5	11	144-154	150-165	159-179
6	0	148-158	154-170	164-184
6	1	152-162	158-175	168-189
6	2	156-167	162-180	173-194
6	3	160-171	167-185	178-199
6	4	164-175	172-190	182-204
with 2" heels		**WOMEN**		
4	10	92- 98	96-107	104-119
4	11	94-101	98-110	106-122
5	0	96-104	101-113	109-125
5	1	99-107	104-116	112-128
5	2	102-110	107-119	115-131
5	3	105-113	110-122	118-134
5	4	108-116	113-126	121-138
5	5	111-119	116-130	125-142
5	6	114-123	120-135	129-146
5	7	118-127	124-139	133-150
5	8	122-131	128-143	137-154
5	9	126-135	132-147	141-158
5	10	130-140	136-151	145-163
5	11	134-144	140-155	149-168
6	0	138-148	144-159	153-173

Picking out a program of exercise is like asking a dozen different men who the most beautiful girl in the world is. One may say Farrah Fawcett, and another

may pick Sophia Loren. Neither is wrong. It is all a
matter of what appeals to you. How you exercise is
not important. What is important is that you exercise
every day, building toward your fitness goal.

I am going to give you a good general exercise
program for a healthy individual between 20 and 45
years of age. This is a program that works for me, and
you can modify it or substitute parts to suit yourself. If
you have had any special medical problems or are
being treated for any medical problem, talk to your
physician and work out with him an exercise
program to fit your needs.

Put on some old clothes and a pair of sneakers and
walk one mile straightaway from your home. Walking
straightaway from your home eliminates cheating
and finding a shortcut on the way back. After two or
three days of this, jog one block and walk one block
for that first mile, then walk home. By the third week
you should be able to alternate walking and jogging
the full two miles without wearing yourself out.
Progress to jogging the full two miles as you feel you
are able, but do not exhaust yourself. It is great for
your wind and your legs. Handball and tennis are
good running substitutes if your prefer to do your
running on a court.

If you have access to weights, lifting is a specific
and definite way to increase strength in arms,
shoulders, legs, and back. Now, you are not getting
ready for the Mr. Universe contest. You are getting
ready to enjoy the outdoors, so don't try to lift the
heaviest possible weight you can. Start with a
manageable weight, say 20 to 40 pounds, and do repeated exercises with that weight. Repetition with
lighter weights will build far greater strength than a
few exhausting attempts with a maximum load. If you
do not have access to weights, you can accomplish the

Demonstration of Isometric Palm Press

same good results with isometric exercises. Isometrics is exerting force against equal counterforce. This can be done as simply as pressing your own palms together. Put your palms together and push them together as hard as you can for ten seconds, release, and repeat ten times. Try this with your hands behind your back. Stand in a doorway and push out with your arms against the frame. Many strength-building isometrics can be done while walking or jogging. Isometrics can be done for ten minutes a day, and you will feel the difference in one week.

Swimming is one of the best general body exercises you can do. It stretches the muscles, builds tone and stamina, and is the best of the limbering exercises I know. If you can get to a pool or lake once a week during your exercise program, do it. If you don't swim, learn how. You owe it to yourself and the other people with whom you hunt and fish.

This whole business of getting back into shape can be completed in about six weeks. It is fun, good for you, and will help you enjoy even more of the things you already enjoy.

Now for some regular doctor talk. You have your mechanic check out your car before you leave on a trip to make sure it won't break down, you have a gunsmith check the guns, and a tackle shop service the reels, but have you checked the only irreplaceable piece of equipment you have—you? Everyone needs a physical examination by a physician once a year, and I can't think of a better time to have it than a week or two before a hunting or fishing trip. If any problems exist, it sure is nice to have them checked and taken care of before your trip and not after they have ruined it. This is also a good time to check to see if your tetanus shots are up to date.

Speaking of checkups, there is another fellow you should stop in on yearly, and that is your family dentist. There are few things that can destroy the pleasure of opening day of the deer season as completely as a toothache. Here again, the time for a dental checkup is a couple of weeks before the trip. These visits can save you a lot of lost hunting and fishing time, and it will make you feel good knowing *all* of your equipment is in good working order.

After getting yourself in shape, you should have a pretty good idea of the limits of your strength and stamina. Stay within your limits, and leave yourself a little reserve. When you function at the edge of endurance, accidents, injuries, and errors in judgement are one hundred times more likely to occur, and one of them might cost you your life.

Being in good shape gives you a very good feeling. Do a friend a favor and get your hunting and fishing partners to join you in the workout and checkup part of trip preparation.

In my opinion, being physically prepared for the outdoors is essential to get the maximum enjoyment available from your hunting and fishing. Once you are in shape, think about this: a regular program of sensible physical exercise will make you feel better, look better, and live longer. Once you have a good thing going, stay with it.

2

Burns

It had been one of those spectacular Ontario mornings—clear sky and warm breezes—and the lake had been very generous with its walleyes. Now, what had been a stringer of glistening gold and black walleyes were golden fillets in bubbling bacon grease. An ideal morning indeed, until Jerry's sleeve caught the handle of the frying pan, and the fillets and boiling grease fell onto his foot and ankle.

The low leather boot had prevented serious injury to the foot, but just above the ankle, there was an angry ring of blisters, redness, and broken skin about 3 inches wide. What would you do for yourself or your best friend in a spot like this? Ice? Ointment? Should you wrap it or leave it open to the air? Should you interrupt the trip to get Jerry to a doctor, or can you safely watch it for a few days yourself? A wrong answer could cost you or your best friend a foot! Let's answer some questions about burns.

Let's talk for just a minute about how a burn—any burn—causes damage. A burn is a surface injury—a thermal injury. Any area of the body which is exposed to a high enough temperature to do damage for a long enough time will be burned. The higher the temperature, the less time you need to be injured, and lower temperatures need more time to cause damage. The longer an area is exposed to the heat, the deeper the burn. Remember that, because it is going to be important when we talk about how to take care of burns.

We are going to define a few important terms in judging how serious a burn is, which will influence how it is to be treated. You probably have heard of first-degree, second-degree, and third-degree burns. Well, I am going to describe them for you.

A first-degree burn is a burn that causes redness of the skin and pain. This is the kind of burn you might get if you were splashed with very hot, but not boiling, water. Most sunburns are first-degree burns. A first-degree burn is the least serious of the burns.

A second-degree burn is a burn that causes blistering of the skin. It is the kind of burn you might get from boiling water, hot grease, or a very bad sunburn. This is more serious than a first-degree burn because it has done deeper damage. If the blisters break, the body's first line of defense against infection, the outer layer of skin, has been broken.

ZONE OF REACTION

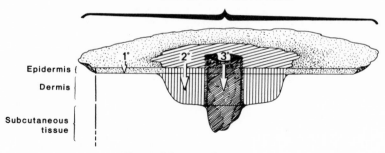

Zone of degree of burns

A third-degree burn is a burn that has completely destroyed the skin and has caused damage beneath the skin. It is the kind of burn that is caused by an open flame or very hot grease. Many chemical burns and almost all electrical burns are third-degree. This is the most serious and most dangerous kind of burn. All layers of the skin are penetrated, with possible damage to nerves, blood vessels, tendons, and muscle.

Beside the degree of a burn, the other factor determining how serious a burn is, is the percentage of total skin area involved. There is a very simple system worked out to estimate the percentage of a burn. It is called the Rule of Nines (see the chart). In an adult the skin of the head and neck is about 9% of the total skin area, each arm is about 9%, the front and back of each leg is 9%, the chest is 9%, the belly is 9%, the upper half of the back is 9%, and the lower half, including the buttocks is 9%. The genital area is approximately 1%. 1% is roughly equal to the palm of the hand. Seriousness of a burn is equal to the degree of the burn plus the percentage of the burn.

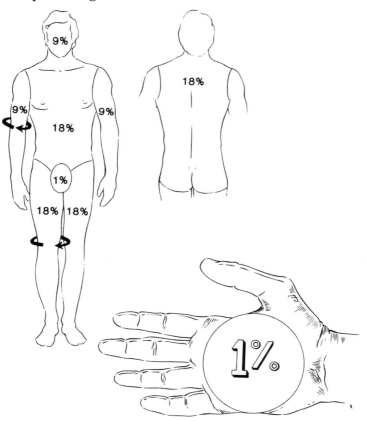

Rule of Nines (hand is 1%)

There are certain areas that require special attention and should be seen by a doctor for any second or third-degree burns; these special areas are the eyes, face, and genitals. Burns in these areas can result in serious scarring or infection if not treated properly. Any burn, generally speaking, of 1% or greater, which is second-degree should be seen by a doctor as soon as possible. Unnecessary delay in receiving treatments can cause serious complications of scarring or infection. Every third-degree burn should be seen by a doctor, regardless of its percentage.

Getting back to Jerry's burn, described at the beginning of the chapter, any second-degree or third-degree burn that completely encircles any part of an arm or leg should be seen by a physician as soon as possible. The swelling that follows a burn of this kind encircling a limb, can be enough to cut off the blood supply and cause loss of the extremity beyond the burn.

Now that you have some background, what should you do if you or someone you're with suffers a burn!

The first step in treating a burn is to *remove the cause*. In the case of thermal injury you have to get the heat out of the burned area by cooling down the burn. This is best done with very cold or iced water. Since burns can get infected and this can cause more damage, add a strong germicidal soap to the iced water. The one I like best is Betadine Liquid Soap, but any germicidal liquid soap will work well. This combination cools and cleans the burn at the same time. A burned hand can be soaked in the solution, or you can soak a cloth in the solution and apply it to the burned area. This should be done for 15 to 30 minutes. If you are taking someone to a doctor, keep the iced soaks on until you get the person there.

If the burn is small (less than 1%), after you have

done 30 minutes of the iced, germicidal soak, dry the area with the cleanest cloth you have available, and using a sterile tongue depressor, spread a very thin layer of germicidal ointment or cream over the entire burned area. The cream I use most often is called Silvadene Cream, but again, there are many good ointments and creams. Have your family doctor recommend the one you should keep in your emergency kit.

After the burn is completely covered by the cream or ointment, dress the burned area completely with a bulky layer of sterile gauze or the cleanest available cloth, and hold the dressing in place with several strips of tape. The burn should be washed with germicidal soap and water three times a day, a fresh layer of cream should be applied, and the burn should be redressed. Try not to handle the part of the gauze or cloth that is going to come directly in contact with the burn.

Following these directions should work well for treating a 1% or smaller first-degree or second-degree burn on someone's arm, chest, back, belly, or leg. First-degree and second-degree burns are very painful; third-degree burns are generally not painful because the nerves have been destroyed by the burn. Most adults can take three or four aspirin or aspirin-substitute tablets and get reasonable pain relief for first-degree or second-degree burns. Dosage directions on bottles should be followed exactly for children.

Burns can occur in an infinite variety of combinations of degree and percentage, and we cannot go over every case. For burns up to 15%, the iced soaks while you get the patient to a doctor will help significantly to prevent infection, pain, and extension of the burn, especially in second-degree burns. In burns of greater than 15% area, especially where skin is lost, loss of body heat is enormous, and the patient should be bundled in two or three blankets or be kept as warm as possible to help prevent shock. Fluid loss is also very great through broken skin, but the only way to help that is to get the burn victim to medical aid as quickly as possible.

Chemical burns, acid or lye, can be evaluated in the same way as thermal burns are evaluated. But the first step with every chemical burn is to flood and wash the burned area with four or five gallons of the cleanest available water as quickly as possible—this is a case where seconds count. Flood the area repeatedly, rinsing all chemicals from the skin surface. From this point forward a chemical burn can be handled similar to a thermal burn.

Electrical burns are among the most insidious of burns, because the electrical injury can be transmitted along nerves and blood vessels and spread its destruction for some distance from the contact site. As we already mentioned, these burns are frequently third-degree. All but the most minor electrical burns should be evaluated and treated by a physician.

Extreme caution when handling gasoline, campfires, tent heaters, and the like is really the best medicine. Even with our most sophisticated hospital burn centers and air ambulances, many people die or suffer disfigurement each year from a high percentage of second-degree and third-degree burns. Please be careful and be prepared.

Let's go over the small list of things you need in your outdoor emergency kit to handle burns properly. They are all available at your pharmacy with your doctor's help.

1. Germicidal liquid soap (Betadine, Germedica, etc.)

2. Sterile gauze packets

3. Sterile tongue depressors

4. Burn ointment or cream (Silvadene, Betadine Ointment, etc.)

5. Tape

With these supplies and the information in this chapter, you should know what to do with burns.

3

Injuries to the Arm and Hand

Joe worked quickly. The blood coming from Ed's forearm, where he had slashed himself accidentally with his skinning knife, wasn't bright red and spurting, but a dull red, oozing mess, still frightening.

Joe's neckerchief easily made the circle around the top of Ed's arm just below the armpit, and Joe cinched it home tightly, just as he had seen the Duke do it so many times.

By the time he'd helped Ed to the RV, Joe was sweating, not because of the exertion but because blood was pouring from the wound, even more than before. Joe tightened his neckerchief tourniquet, using a piece of wood under it as a windlass, secured the wood with several pieces of twine, and removed the bloodsoaked dressing he had first put on Ed's forearm. The bleeding had now stopped.

Four hours later, in the hospital, an anxious surgeon rapidly removed the tourniquet and breathed a sigh of relief as Ed's white hand slowly became pink. However, the numbness in Ed's arm, which had started after Joe had windlassed the tourniquet, didn't recover, and the surgeon was able to deal with the wound without having to give an anesthetic.

Six months later the feeling in Ed's arm had improved but wasn't normal and his grip was still weak; he told Joe that he didn't think he would be doing any hunting the next season.

This unhappy story could have had a happier ending if Joe had had a chance to read this book. But you're the lucky one because you're about to share some time with Robert (BUCKIN') Chesney, M.D.

25

F.R.C.S., hunter, fisherman, and orthopedic surgeon, (formerly at Rush-Presbyterian-St. Luke's Medical Center), whose special area of expertise is surgery of the arm and hand. Dr. Chesney's—sorry—Buckin's hometown is Aberdeen, Scotland. So put on your kilt and let's join him for a pint at the wee pub near his favorite trout stream and listen to his experienced words on injuries to the arm and hand.

The hunting Eds of this world can take some consolation from the knowledge that the only injury of the upper limb that is immediately life-threatening is a partial division of a major artery. Steady pressure *directly* on the bleeding point for 10 to 15 minutes will always control bleeding.

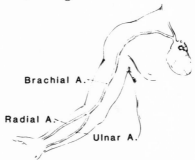

Location of major artieres in the arm

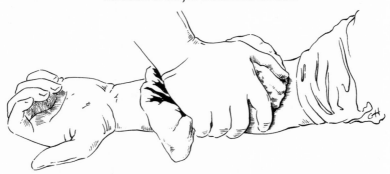

Avoid Tourniquets—Apply direct pressure to wound for control of bleeding

The hunting Joes need to avoid doing things that cause permanent damage. The only place for the tourniquet is the operating room—the broad inflatable surgical tourniquet can be set accurately to correct pressures. The various bandages, neckties, and other assorted devices pressed into emergency service as tourniquets are *very* dangerous—often they are applied at a pressure sufficient to obstruct blood outflow (venous) from the limb but insufficient to prevent blood inflow (arterial). The result is that blood continues to flow into the limb, and its only way out is through the cut ends of veins in wounds, so that blood loss increases instead of lessening.

If the emergency tourniquet has been applied with sufficient pressure to stop arterial inflow, often the pressure exerted will be excessive and will cause direct pressure damage—often permanent—to important nerves, as in Ed's case. The narrow width of these tourniquets accentuates this total nerve damage.

If the tourniquets are left on too long, say more than three hours, both muscles and nerves may be permanently damaged from the absence of blood supply.

In short, tourniquets should *never* be used in the field; they are dangerous and unnecessary. Direct firm pressure over a bleeding area for 10 to 15 minutes will always control the blood loss. If you carry a hemostat and use it as a fishhook remover, never try to clamp a wound bleeder—you'll probably clamp an important nerve instead. The hand is the unique power and precision tool on which we depend and which is most often damaged in upper-limb injuries. The rest of the upper extremity is basically a multijointed lever system designed to put the hand "on the job." So we must be careful to avoid doing anything that could damage hand function.

Simple skin wounds are frequent, superficial, clean; incised wounds require no more than a thorough wash and a simple clean dressing. Flesh and tear wounds are more serious, especially if they are extensive and important deep structures like tendons and nerves are exposed. Such wounds should be covered with a clean dressing soaked in germicidal solution, and the victim should be taken to the nearest emergency room. The hunter who carries tapes or even sutures should never attempt to close such a wound, which needs full exploration and removal of dirty and dead tissue under operating room conditions.

Appearance of hand in a relaxed state

Tendon and nerve damage in the hand can easily be missed. Look at your own hand as it lies relaxed—the tip of your thumb slightly bent, the whole thumb stands off from the palm, and the other digits are bent, the degree of flexion (bending toward the palm) being progressively more from the index finger through to the little finger.

In the thumb one long flexor tendon runs up the joint and bends the end joint; the next joint up is bent by one of the small muscles in the ball of the thumb—that is the group of muscles that lifts the thumb away from the palm. The other digits have two long flexor tendons; a deep one that runs out to bend the end joint next to the nail and a superficial one that bends the joint in the middle of the finger. On the back of the thumb a long extensor tendon pulls the end joint straight and a short extensor tendon straightens the next joint up.

The long extensor tendons of the other fingers run all the way out to the area of the root of the nail. This extensor mechanism on the back and sides of each finger is complex. The important thing to realize is that the long extensor tendon in each finger (you can see these tendons moving on the back of your hand when you wiggle your fingers) has the principal job of straightening the knuckle joint. The two joints in the finger are straightened by little muscles deep in the palm that send their tendons out onto the back of the finger. Small muscles deep in the hand are responsible for moving the fingers sideways, together and apart.

When you have to deal with a hunting friend who has a deep cut on the front of the wrist or on the front of a finger, look at the position of the fingers. If there is a finger that lies completely straight in the relaxed position and has lost its natural flexed attitude, that's good presumptive evidence that the flexor tendons have been completely severed. The opposite doesn't apply, however. A finger that still lies flexed may have one tendon completely cut and the other partially divided.

The flexor tendons can be tested individually in the following way.

Fix the thumb knuckle joint straight with your fingers and ask the injured person to bend the tip joint; if the person can't do it, the flexor tendon is severed.

In turn, fix the joint in the middle of each of the other digits and ask that the tip be bent. This tests the deep flexor tendons. Next, hold the middle, ring, and little fingers straight and ask your friend to bend the joint in the middle of the index finger. This tests the superficial tendon. It's necessary to hold the other three digits straight so as to stop the deep flexor tendon from moving the middle joint and giving a false result.

Now repeat this for the middle, ring, and little fingers in turn, remembering to hold the other three straight. Note that some normal people (including me) do not have a superficial tendon to the little finger and are unable to bend its middle joint with the other fingers held straight. Examination of the opposite hand might give the clue that this is a normal situation, but only proper exploration of the wound in the hospital will definitely provide the answer. The most common place for the extensor tendon to be severed is over the back of the hand. To test them, ask that the knuckles be straightened. The index and little fingers have additional extensor tendons; these can be tested by asking that the fingers be individually straightened while the other digits are kept bunched in a fist.

Note that in all tendon testing the absence of a particular movement implies a severed tendon, but the presence of a particular movement does not imply that the tendon is completely intact — it may be nine-tenths severed. Tendons should always be repaired as quickly as possible in a hospital to get the best results. Severed tendons that have been neglected can be reconstructed, but such surgery is more involved, may require several weeks off work, and will not usually give as good results as primary repair carried out by a good surgeon.

The hand is served by three main nerves. The largest one, the *median nerve*, runs down the middle of the front of the forearm and wrist and gets into the hand through a tunnel roofed over by a tough fibrous ligament. On the palm side of the muscle mass that makes up the ball of the thumb, a very important branch comes off the median nerve. This branch motors the muscles in the ball of the thumb, making it possible for the thumb to be lifted away from the palm and rotated round to oppose the other digits. This movement is basic to the unique function of the thumb. Deep wounds in the region of this important motor branch must be explored under hospital conditions.

After giving off this motor branch, the median nerve splits into branches that give sensation to the front of the thumb, index, and middle fingers and to the thumb half of the front of the ring finger.

The median nerve is a common casualty of deep lacerations over the front of the wrist. In such a case you will see the thumb lying flat against the palm like an ape's thumb. This position is due to the paralysis of the muscles of the ball of the thumb, which normally keep the thumb up and away from the palm. Testing the sensory territory of this nerve, e.g., over the front of the index finger, with a safety pin will show blunting of sensation compared to the opposite normal index and will confirm the suspicion of median nerve division.

The second largest nerve is the *ulnar nerve*. This enters the hand on the little finger side of the front of the wrist. It supplies sensation to the front of the little finger and the little finger half of the ring finger, but its most important function is to motor the majority of the many small muscles inside the hand (intrinsic muscles), which are responsible for much of the delicate, manipulative, precision skills of the hand. This nerve is frequently divided in wrist wounds, as is the median. Its function can be tested by asking the victim to spread the straight fingers apart and to resist trying to push the little finger sideways towards the ring finger. Testing the front of the little finger with a safety pin will show blunting of sensation. The digital branches of both median and ulnar nerves are commonly divided in finger wounds. A digital branch runs up the front of each side of a finger and immediately deep to it lies a digital artery. This can give a clue in finger wounds. If you see a finger wound spurting blood on one side, the chances are high that its accompanying nerve is divided, since the wounding instrument, usually entering the front of the finger, has to pass through the nerve to get to the artery. Sensation beyond the finger wound will be blunted; commonly there will be tendon damage as well.

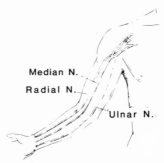

Median N.

Radial N.

Ulnar N.

Location of major nerves in the arm or forearm

The third hand nerve is the *radial*. It enters the hand on the side of the wrist in line with the thumb, closely related to the knob of wrist bone there. Its function is purely to supply sensation over two thirds of the back of the hand, over the whole of the back of the thumb, and the first half of the back of the index and middle fingers. Its importance is that sometimes it gives sensation round on the front of the thumb tip where good sensation is important, and that when divided at wrist level and untreated, it can give rise to painful nerve lumps (neuromas). It can be tested by checking sensation in its territory beyond the wound.

Fractures and dislocations in the hand are usually obvious, with pain, swelling, deformity, and loss of function. Many sportsmen reduce their own finger dislocations, but some dislocations are complex and need operative reduction. All fractures and dislocations (if already reduced) should be promptly seen in an emergency room. Emergency splintage is best confined to soft, bulky dressings bandaged loosely in place; the hand should be ideally positioned with wrist back, knuckles at 90 degrees, finger joints straight, and thumb straight and moved away from the palm. The injured hand must be elevated to minimize swelling. The simplest sling is improvised from the hunter's shirt or jersey. Assuming a left-hand injury, the left front part of the shirt is pulled over the elbow and pinned below the left shoulder, thus supporting the elbow; the right front part of the shirt is pulled over the forearm and pinned near the left collar. The injured person during this process supports their left hand against their right shoulder.

Arm secured to the body—sling positioned

Open fractures, i.e., fractures with overlying skin wounds allowing direct communication between the fracture and the atmosphere, require particularly prompt hospital attention to clean and close the wound. The break in th skin should be covered with sterile dressing soaked ir germicidal soap until help is reached.

One fracture of the hand with a well-deserved reputation for trouble in later years, if neglected, is the fracture of the scaphoid (navicular). This is acquired by falling on the outstretched hand. Pain is felt in the wrist area, and tenderness is found in the anatomical snuffbox-the concavity on the back of the wrist at the root of the thumb. Sometimes initial x-rays do not show the fracture, but the presence of tenderness over the bone is a sound indication for a cast. Further x-rays taken 10 days later will show the fracture. Any sportsman who falls in this way and has tenderness in his snuffbox should not delay going to an emergency room. If untreated, this fracture can lead to painful arthritis of the wrist.

Fractures of the arm bone (humerus), forearm bones (radius and ulna), and the wrist are best immobilized by bulky soft dressings, such as shirts and jerseys. Even soft dressings like this, if bulky enough, will significantly reduce movement and pain. To give added rigidity, a few longitudinally placed twigs can be taped on top of the dressings.

Open fractures should have the cleanest available dressing placed over the wound. Dislocations of shoulder and elbow are sometimes reduced in the field, and this is a dangerous practice — without an x-ray it can be impossible to tell whether there is a fracture associated with the dislocation. At both shoulder and elbow important vessels and nerves pass close to the joints. Unskilled manipulation puts these structures at risk.

With fractures, dislocations, and deep wounds of

the upper limb, always check the circulation. If the hand is pale and no pulses can be felt at the wrist, this is an urgent situation. Waste no time in getting your companion to a hospital where torn, crushed, or compressed major arteries can be treated and circulation restored.

One dramatic injury of the upper limb that microsurgical techniques have made it possible to treat is amputation of a part. If your companion chops off a thumb (or any other major part of anatomy), do not panic. With a dressing apply firm pressure for 10 minutes to the bleeding stump. Leave the injured person to continue holding the dressing and pick up the amputated thumb. If it has fallen in mud or dirt, wash it gently with your canteen water or in a stream. Next put it in a plastic bag, if you have one, if not, in a moistened towel or thick piece of cloth. If you have been enjoying a luxury hunting trip, pack ice around the plastic bag or towel in any suitable container. If you have no ice, get some at the nearest farmhouse or village.

Never put ice directly against the amputated thumb, which has to be cooled but not frozen. Once you have cooled the thumb, you have bought yourself several hours in which to get your friend to a hospital that has a microsurgical service. Next day, with any luck, your friend's thumb should be back where it belongs and looking "in the pink."

Suggested material for a long hunting trip:

4 safety pins (to secure slings)

4 packs 4 x 4 sterile dressings

Pack bulky sterile dressing pads

Kerlix roll

2 aluminum finger splints

4

Leg Injuries

You hear a gunshot ahead and come across your friend who has accidentally shot himself through the thigh. He is lying on the ground, with the jagged end of a bone sticking out of the wound. Blood is spurting three or four feet into the air. What do you do? This chapter will attempt to answer this and other questions.

This grisly but accurate description of an accidental rifle shot to the thigh is given by an orthopedic trauma surgeon—John M. Jones, M.D., F.R.C.S., (formerly of Rush-Presbyterian-St. Luke's Medical Center). When Dr. Jones isn't handling the orthopedic traumas around Cardiff, South Wales, you'll find him searching for sea trout along the Dee River in South Wales. So let's join Dr. Jones on the bank of the Dee and gather in his good advice on injuries of the lower limb.

Soft Tissue Injuries

Most injuries involve soft tissues, which include the skin and muscles. Such injuries may be open or closed. An open wound is one in which there is a break in the skin; a closed wound means that the damage occurs beneath the skin, but there is no break in the overlying skin.

Open Wounds

Open wounds are easily recognized because they bleed. Since the skin has been damaged, these wounds are easily contaminated and may become infected. There are various types of open wounds, such as abrasions, lacerations, avulsions, and puncture wounds.

An abrasion can be sustained if the leg is scraped against a rock or tree. The outer part of the skin is damaged, and the wound will ooze blood and be painful.

A knife or piece of glass will produce a laceration, which will cut right through the skin and may also damage deeper muscles, blood vessels, or nerves. If a blood vessel is damaged, there can be a considerable amount of bleeding. Two types of blood vessels can be involved: if a vein is cut, the blood will not usually squirt out and will be darker than if an artery is cut, in which case bright blood will pump out and cause serious or even fatal blood loss if the hemorrhage is not controlled quickly. If a nerve is cut, the patient may be unable to move or feel his leg below the wound.

An avulsion is a wound in which a portion of skin and possibly underlying muscle is torn off by being caught, for example, on a sharp spike or a nail. It may be torn off completely or left hanging by one edge. If possible, the part that is completely torn or cut off should be kept and cooled in ice or snow, as it is sometimes possible to stitch it back on later.

The skin may be punctured by various objects, such as a nail or thorn entering the foot, or by an accidental gunshot wound.

TREATMENT OF OPEN WOUNDS

There are three things to do if someone has sustained a severe open wound: (1) control bleeding, (2) prevent contamination and possible infection later, and (3) immobilize the part.

1. *Control Bleeding*—A bullet wound of the inside of the thigh can easily divide the main artery of the leg. The bleeding will be torrential, and if it is

not controlled rapidly, will probably be fatal. How does one stop this bleeding?

Local pressure on the bleeding point—with the bare hand or fist if necessary—will normally stop even the most severe bleeding. To maintain this compression, a sterile dressing or clean handkerchief should be put over the wound and covered with a wad of material, such as a rolled-up shirt or towel, bandaged firmly to the leg. If bleeding does not stop, tighten the bandage some more or add more dressings to the ones you have already put on.

If this does not work, then you can press firmly on an arterial pressure point.

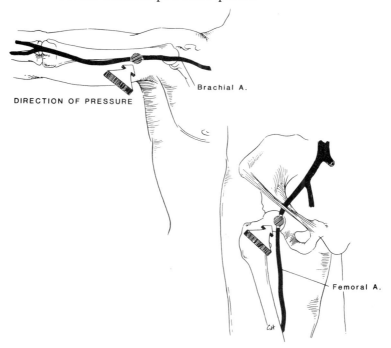

Location of two major pressure points

They can be identified by feeling the underlying pulsation. The most important one is the femoral artery in the groin, which is about one third of the way across the groin. Firm pressure here will diminish bleeding from any leg wound. Pressure over the inside of the ankle will only stop bleeding from a wound in the foot.

2. *Prevent contamination*—As mentioned, the wound should be covered with a clean dressing soaked in antiseptic solution, e.g., Betadine solution. Cut away nearby clothing. Don't try to remove trousers normally, as this will produce unnecessary pain and also cause movement that may increase the bleeding. Don't remove material from inside the wound for the same reason. This applies also to impaled objects, such as a knife or a piece of wood or metal, the removal of which could cause additional damage to nerves and blood vessels. Also, don't press on an object sticking out of the wound. Shorten it if this is necessary to make transportation of the patient easier, but protect the protruding part surrounding it with bulky dressings.

3. *Immobilize*—The injured person will be more comfortable, and the bleeding will be diminished if you prevent movement of the injured area. In the leg, one way of doing this is to bind the injured leg firmly to the uninjured one. In regards to the foot or ankle, a pillow or other similar object can be folded around both sides of the ankle from the sole of the foot and held in place with bandages, such as Kerlix rolls. If you don't have bandages, tear a shirt into strips.

Application of soft bulky objects to immobilize injured ankle

I hear an increasing clamor of voices, shouting. "What about a tourniquet to stop the bleeding?" Tourniquets are *dangerous*, even lethal, and should be used only as a last resort. Adequate local pressure over the wound or over the femoral pressure point in the groin and immobilization of the part will virtually always stop bleeding from the leg. If a tourniquet has to be applied, *never* put one on below the knee, as this can cause irreparable damage to nerves and arteries; don't loosen it until a doctor has seen the victim, as this could release lethal poisons into the bloodstream; don't hide it from view, but put some sort of label on the injured person to show that a tourniquet has been applied—ideally, mark his forehead indelibly with the letters TK and the time. If you do have to put a tourniquet on, which is most likely if the leg has been amputated, use at least six layers of a wide bandage, such as a Kerlix roll; wrap it twice around the thigh as close to the wound as possible, tie one knot in the bandage, place a stick or a metal rod on top of the knot, and then tie a square knot over the stick. The stick can then be twisted to tighten the tourniquet and be secured in place.

Closed Wounds

A fall against a rock or a tree stump, for instance, may produce an injury that does not penetrate the skin. This sort of injury is called a *closed wound*. Tissue beneath the skin is crushed and reacts by leaking fluid or blood, which causes swelling and perhaps visible bruising.

TREATMENT OF CLOSED WOUNDS

A small bruise clearly requires no specific treatment, but a large bruise, apart from being extremely painful, can be much more serious. It can even produce loss of blood pressure and faintness, and in such a situation an underlying fracture should be suspected. Swelling can be prevented to a certain extent by applying a pressure bandage, as previously described for stopping bleeding from an open wound. A cold compress is also helpful and soothing, and if the injury is severe, a splint can be applied. A good maxim is: "If in doubt, splint." If put on correctly, the splint will certainly do no harm. Splinting is described under "Closed Fractures."

Fractures

A fracture is a broken bone. The bone may be only cracked, or the pieces of bone may be separated, making the fracture easy to recognize because of the abnormal motion or position of the leg or foot.

A fracture can be sustained in many different ways. One of the most common fractures in the leg is an ankle fracture, which can easily happen if the foot gets caught in a rabbit hole or is put down unexpectedly on uneven ground. The body twists on the fixed foot, and if the twist is sufficiently forceful, the ankle will break. In this case the victim will fall as a result of the fracture. Frequently, however, a fracture results from a fall. A severe fall can result in a fracture of any bone in the leg, including the pelvis, the thigh bone (femur), the tibia (the shin bone), the fibula (outside the shin bone), or any bone in the foot. Also, a direct fall on the point of the knee can fracture the kneecap.

Powerful muscle contractions can also cause fractures. For example, the toe of a boot might catch while a person is walking over uneven ground. The forward momentum of the body causes the powerful muscles in the front of the thigh to contract in an attempt to prevent the victim from falling forward. When this happens, particularly in .older people, the kneecap may be literally pulled apart. As in most fractures of the leg, walking will then be completely out of the question because the pain will be severe, and it will prove impossible to lift the leg.

An unaccustomed long hike can also lead to stress fractures. A small bone in the foot or the fibula itself may crack and produce pain. Apart from the pain, which can often be controlled by analgesics, stress fractures are unimportant and don't require any special treatment except for a bandage to minimize swelling and occasionally a cast simply to lessen the pain.

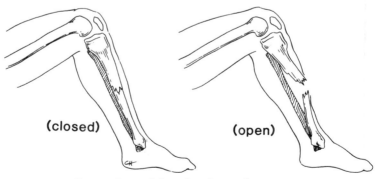

(closed)   (open)

Comparison of closed and open fractures

Fractures are either closed (simple) or open (compound). In a closed fracture the skin has not been lacerated or been penetrated by the bone ends. In an open fracture, the bone has broken through the skin or there is an accompanying wound that extends through the skin to the broken bone.

CLOSED FRACTURES

Although some fractures can only be recognized by an appropriate x-ray examination, many can be easily identified or at least strongly suspected by simple inspection.

A person's legs are normally symmetrical; if an injured leg looks deformed, suspect a fracture.

If a middle-aged or elderly person falls, a hip fracture may be sustained. The leg will look short and will be rotated outwards, so that the kneecap points away from the other leg. A fracture of the femur produces deformity of the thigh; the thigh may be bent abnormally and will also be swollen. A fracture of the kneecap will cause swelling in front of the knee, and it will appear that the front of the knee is too high. If the foot points in or out and this is associated with swelling and deformity of the ankle, suspect a fractured ankle.

Swelling to some degree is almost always present with fractures. If a swelling develops quickly, there is likely to be internal bleeding. Whereas, if swelling occurs after several hours, it is probably due to edema (leakage of fluid into the surrounding soft tissues). A fracture will be painful and tender, and movement may produce a grating feeling. This sign should not be intentially sought, however, as trying to find it only increases pain and may cause more damage. Usually the person will also be unable to put any weight on the leg.

It is important to find out if the victim has normal feeling and circulation below the site of the fracture. If you suspect a fracture in the thigh and the leg below the knee looks white and feels cold, the main artery may have been damaged. This means there is no circulation below the fracture. In such a case it is very important to get the person to a hospital as rapidly as possible.

OPEN FRACTURES

An open fracture is like a closed fracture except that the skin and soft tissue over the fracture have been lacerated. This can happen if someone falls against a hard object with sufficient force both to cut the skin and break the bone, or if the fracture has angulated so much that the sharp ends of the bone cut through the skin from the inside. In either case you may be able to see bone fragments in the depth of the wound.

TREATMENT OF LEG FRACTURES

Avoid unnecessary movement by cutting trousers off rather than removing them normally. Try to decide if there is normal feeling and circulation below the fracture.

If there is a deformity caused by the leg being bent or twisted abnormally, try to correct this by pulling gently in a straight line on the foot or ankle. Never try simply to bend the leg back into shape, because this can cause a lot of internal damage. The leg should be pulled slowly and gently over a few minutes (rather than rapidly) and then only if it is not excessively painful. If you see that bone ends are lying just under intact skin, be careful that they don't cut through the skin, as this would convert the fracture into an open one, which would be more likely to get infected later. If bone ends are sticking out of a wound, never try to push them back inside. If they do go back in spon-

taneously while you are pulling, make a note of this
so that the doctor will know that there is likely to be
considerable contamination inside the wound.
Always cover the break in the skin with sterile dressing soaked in antiseptic solution.

Splinting technique for leg injury
Splint will immobilize the entire leg

When the leg is in as good a position as possible,
put on a splint. The injured leg can be bound firmly to
the good leg, or a splint can be improvised by using
clothes to pad, straight pieces of wood or branches, or
even a gun, and binding this with bandages to the
outside of the leg. For a fractured ankle, use something like a pillow wrapped around the foot and held
in place with bandages. Never try to move the victim
until the fracture has been splinted.

If the fracture is open (compound), the wound
should be treated as previously described under
"Treatment of Open Wounds."

Remember that a fracture, even if closed, usually
bleeds more than a soft tissue wound. The amount of
blood lost is variable, but a rule of thumb is that a
fractured pelvis loses 3 pints, a fractured femur 2
pints, and a tibia 1 pint. The loss of even 2 pints of
blood is serious. Stop external bleeding from an open
wound by local pressure or pressure over the groin
pressure point.

The victim who has lost 2 pints of blood, or even 'ss, can go into shock. Their skin will be cold and clammy. Their eyes will be dull, and the pupils may be large. The victim will be anxious and thirsty. Don't give the person food or fluid, as this may cause vomiting. Breathing will be shallow and rapid. Pulse will be weak, meaning that the circulation is poor. This can be improved by raising the feet 12 inches (making sure that the injured leg is properly splinted) and keeping the head low. Keep the patient warm, comfortable, and handle gently.

Dislocations

A dislocation means that a joint has come out of place. The bone ends forming the joint have moved out of position so that the joint surfaces are no longer in proper contact. A dislocated joint will be deformed and swollen. Attempted movement will be painful. Although any joint can dislocate, most common in the leg is a dislocation of the kneecap, which displaces to the outside of the knee. Treatment consists of gently pulling on the lower part of the leg so that the knee straightens. The kneecap may pop back into place on its own. If the leg won't straighten completely, don't force it — put on a splint in the best position obtained.

Sprains

Joints are held together by ligaments. In a sprain these ligaments are stretched or torn, but not severely enough for the joint to dislocate. The ankle is the most common joint to be sprained; usually the foot is turned inward, causing pain and swelling on the outside of the ankle. The same thing can happen to the inside of the knee. A sprain should be treated by firm bandaging. A minor sprain does not prevent walking, but a serious one requires hospital treatment.

Equipment

The following are useful things to have with you.

1. One universal dressing (9" x 36") to use as pressure dressing
2. Adhesive dressing such as Band Aids
3. Four 4" x 4" sterile gauze pads
4. One 5-yard Kerlix roll
5. Antiseptic solution such as Betadine
6. One 4" elastic bandage

Before your trip, Dr. Jones reminds you to make sure you are immunized against tetanus.

5

Head and Spinal Cord Injuries

Fortunately, severe disorders or dysfunction of the brain, spinal cord, or nerves are encountered infrequently by the outdoor sportsman. Head bumps and back strains are common but usually do not require sophisticated facilities for treatment. Severe injuries, however, are often fatal unless the victim is rapidly and correctly managed at emergency medical facilities. Knowledge of the symptoms and consequences of trivial and intermediate injuries is most important to the sportsman. An insignificant head injury may be the sentinel of more extensive intracranial pathology, which if left unattended, could be fatal or result in permanent neurological disability. It therefore behooves the sportspersons to familiarize themselves with certain disorders of the nervous system and their symptoms, since this familiarity may mean the difference between normal neurological function and severe neurological deficit.

The woods of New England with their brook-trout-filled streams are the favorite places of Charles D'Angelo, M.D. Charlie, formerly a spinal cord researcher at Yale, is now transplanted to Chicago, where he is Associate Professor of Neurological Surgery and Associate Attending Physician at Rush-Presbyterian-St. Luke's Medical Center. His love of the Outdoors and neurological surgery made him the natural choice to tell us about head and spinal trauma. Okay, if you're ready, grab your fly rod, put on your waders, and let's step into the stream next to Charlie and listen to him tell us about head and spine injuries in the outdoors.

Turban Head dressing. Notice that the dressing does
not cover the ear

Scalp Wounds

Scalp wounds encompass contusions, abrasions,
and lacerations. A contusion is an area of swollen
ecchymotic (black-and-blue) tissue. A simple contusion is usually of little neurological significance other
than indicating the mechanism of a head injury or
raising suspicion of an underlying skull fracture
(which we shall discuss later). The pain and swelling
of a contusion may be reduced by directly applying ice
packs or cold packs to the area of injury. The pain is
also eased by taking aspirin, two pills every 5 to 6
hours as needed.

A break in the skin in the area of an injury, such as
a contusion, constitutes an abrasion. Abrasions have
the same neurological significance as contusions. The
area of injury should be cleaned with cool or
lukewarm water. Ointments or salves should not be
applied to the abrasion. Pain management is the same
as for contusions.

Scalp lacerations can be severe, resulting in profuse
bleeding. Superficial lacerations do not require any
special treatment and can be managed like abrasions.
Deeper or longer lacerations should be cleaned with
water and dressed with gauze and adhesive tape before the individual is taken to a nearby physician. Severe lacerations with hemorrhage can be difficult to

manage. The wound should not be probed. Hemorrhage can be decreased by applying finger pressure to the skin edges bounding the laceration. If an emergency kit is available, the laceration should be covered with gauze and a turban-type head dressing applied. If no emergency kit is available, the laceration should be covered with a clean handkerchief, and then a turban-type headdress may be made from a T-shirt cut into strips measuring three or four inches wide. The patient should then be taken to the nearest medical facility.

Head Injuries

CEREBRAL CONCUSSION

The temporary loss of consciousness following a blow to the head is termed a cerebral concussion. The victim is "knocked out." By definition there is no structural or pathological damage to the brain. The blow to the head, sometimes trivial, causes a temporary cessation of brain-cell activity.

The duration of unconsciousness may be a few seconds or many minutes. The time a person remains unconscious is usually overestimated by observers. Upon regaining consciousness, the individual is usually confused and disoriented. Headache and a complaint that light "bothers the eyes" are not infrequent. Often the victim cannot recall events that preceded the head injury. What was eaten for breakfast or lunch on the day of the injury may be completely forgotten. At times the individual has no remembrance of activities for many days preceding the concussive injury. This forgetting of events preceding a concussion is called retrograde amnesia and is an important piece of neurological history. Many neurologists and neurosurgeons think there is a positive correlation between the degree of concussion and the duration of retrograde amnesia — that is, the more severe the concussion, the greater the period of retrograde amnesia.

Usually a concussion alone is not a serious neurological condition. Its occurrence does, however, indicate that the brain has been dealt a significant blow and compels us to be wary of other neurological problems — namely, skull fractures, cerebral contusions, or intracranial hemorrhages. All persons sustaining a cerebral concussion should be evaluated by a physician as soon as possible and observed for 24 to 48 hours. In the wilderness such an evaluation is not always possible. If travel to a medical facility is impractical, the victim should still be carefully observed for 48 hours. Nothing should be taken by mouth except water for 8 hours. After regaining consciousness, the individual should be examined carefully for the following signs, which have ominous importance and demand immediate medical attention:

1. Progressive confusion, disorientation, or sleepiness

2. Increasing intensity of headaches

3. Unequal pupils or double vision

4. Vomiting

5. Weakness of any limb

The person sustaining a head injury may be allowed to sleep, but the observer should awaken the individual every 60 minutes. The person should be easily aroused and exhibit appropriate responses when awakened. A physician should be sought if the person fails to awaken easily.

CEREBRAL CONTUSION

A bruised brain is a cerebral contusion. Whenever the skull is struck, it rotates, and so does the brain within it. At times the brain can be bruised where it rotates against bony protuberance on the inner table of the skull. Like a contusion anywhere in the body, the area of cerebral contusion becomes ecchymotic and swollen.

The symptoms and signs of cerebral contusion usually begin like those of cerebral concussion. The warning signs discussed in the section on cerebral concussion usually develop. Again, it is very important to watch for these warning signs. A cerebral contusion is a medical emergency.

INTRACRANIAL HEMORRHAGE

Intracranial hemorrhages include epidural hematomas, subdural hematomas, and intracerebral hematomas. Hematoma is a collection of blood.

The mass of an epidural hematoma occurs beneath the skull but over the surface of the brain membranes. It usually is due to a lacerated artery following a skull fracture. The expanding mass of blood, under arterial pressure, develops rapidly and compresses the brain. Epidural hematomas are fatal if not surgically decompressed. The warning signs discussed previously develop rapidly. Epidural hematoma is a neurosurgical emergency!

Acute subdural hematomas occur outside actual brain tissue but beneath the membranes covering the brain. Unlike epidural hematomas, subdural hematomas arise from torn veins. Because venous pressure is lower than arterial pressure, the mass of the subdural hematoma, and consequently the warning signs we have discussed, develop more slowly.

However, the mass is no less lethal if not surgically decompressed. Any patient suspected of having a subdural hematoma must be seen by a physician immediately.

Intracerebral hematomas occur when forces disrupt brain tissue and vessels so that bleeding occurs within the substance of the brain. The expanding mass adds volume to the intracranial vault and compresses the surrounding normal brain. Warning signs develop as in other intracranial hematomas. Surgical decompression is usually required.

Any injured person with an expanding cranial mass (acute epidural hematoma, acute subdural hematoma, or acute intracerebral hematoma), should be taken to an emergency medical facility immediately. During transportation the person's airway should be free of secretions or vomitus. The head should be elevated higher than chest level. Nothing should be taken by mouth.

Skull Fractures

A blow to the skull sufficient to disrupt its bony integrity results in a skull fracture. Missile injuries, falls, or blows to the head, some often trivial, may cause a skull fracture. Except in compound fractures, in which bony disruption can be visualized through the scalp laceration, skull fractures are detected by radiography—x-rays. A skull fracture should be suspected following any head injury but especially if one observes ecchymosis (black and blue) behind the ear (Battle's sign), from the ear canal. Any individual suspected of having a skull fracture should be evaluated by a physician.

A bloody, watery discharge or clear discharge from the nostril or ear canal may indicate a special type of skull fracture, a basal skull fracture. Basal skull fractures are especially serious, since they may precede cerebral meningitis. Such fractures require immediate medical evaluation.

Convulsions

A convulsion, also known as a seizure, "fit," or epileptic attack, is an uncontrolled, involuntary continued muscular movement. Often the attack is preceded by an aura described as a "strange feeling," "butterflies in my stomach," or staring. The aura, if it occurs, is followed by jerking, almost rhythmic movements in the face, arms, or legs, with eventual involvement of all muscles. During the attack, consciousness is usually lost and the victim becomes cyanotic (turns blue) because respirations temporarily cease. Loss of urine control is not unusual. The involuntary motor activities may be so violent as to cause compression fractures of the spinal vertebrae. Upon regaining consciousness, the stricken individual may complain of headache, muscle pain, or back pain. The patient is often temporarily confused. At times, there may be paralysis of the face, arm, or leg on the same side.

Although the causes of convulsions are legion, the underlying mechanism is the same—irritation of the brain surface or cortex. In individuals with no history of previous convulsions, the cause may be a head injury, brain tumor, vascular malformation of the brain, brain hemorrhage, infection, low blood sugar, disturbances of water-salt balance, or one of many other disorders that require neurological evaluation for discovery. Individuals with known seizure disorders may have failed to take their anticonvulsive medications or consumed too much alcohol, or may be harboring an undiagnosed infection.

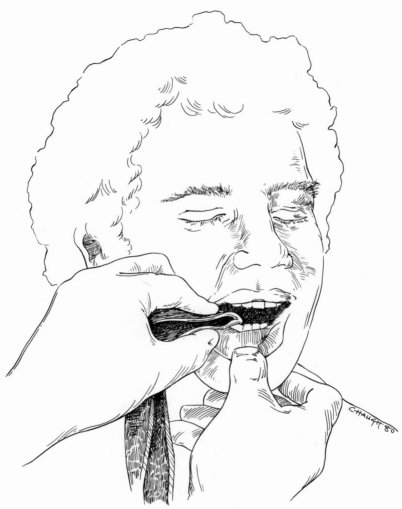

Placement of folded belt in mouth during convulsion or seizure

Management of convulsions is divided into emergency and preventive measures. During the chonic stage of a convulsion, when involuntary jerking movements are occurring, no attempt to restrain the individual should be made, since such restraint may promote further injuries. Care should be taken to prevent falls or self-injury by knocking over objects, breaking glass, etc. The shirt collar should be loosened, and if possible, lacerations of the tongue and cheek by jerking movements of the jaw should be minimized by placing a firm, but not hard object between the teeth. A belt folded on itself or a knife scabbard are usually available and work well. When muscle activity has ceased, the unconscious individual should be turned on a side and vomitus and other debris removed from the mouth. No attempt should be made to force water or "stimulants" into the mouth of an unconscious patient. Once the seizure is over, the individual should be taken to the nearest medical facility for a definitive evaluation and therapy.

Strokes

A cerebral vascular accident (CVA, or stroke) is the term applied to the sudden cessation of blood flow to a part of the brain, resulting in its dysfunction or destruction. The person suddenly may be unable to speak, see on one side, or move an arm, a leg, or the face. An acute cerebral vascular accident requires immediate medical attention.

Neck Injuries

ACUTE CERVICAL STRAIN

Injuries to the cervical spine (neck area) and its supporting muscles may be obvious, such as those following a blow to the head or neck, or a "whiplash" following a fall. Often the injury is trivial and cannot be recalled. Following an uneventful sleep, the individual may awaken with an acute cervical strain.

Regardless of the nature of the cervical strain, the symptoms are often the same. The victim experiences pain, ache, or stiffness (cervical spasm) in the back of the neck. The subjective symptoms often radiate into the back of the head, or the shoulders or between the shoulder blades. The head cannot be turned side to side or moved forward or backward because of stiffness, or is not moved because of pain.

The pain of acute cervical sprain may be lessened by applying warm, moist towels to the back of the neck or by restricting movement of the neck or head. Restriction can be accomplished in the out-of-doors or in camp by taking a towel or flannel shirt and folding it to measure approximately 4 inches wide and 12 to 18 inches long. The folded cloth should be wrapped around the neck and be secured with safety pins. The folded towel or shirt should fit snugly between the jaw and the chest and comfortably restrict forward or backward movement, as well as side tilting and rotation, of the head. Muscle relaxation may be facilitated by application of warm towels and the occasional ingestion of 2 to 4 ounces of whiskey. Every effort should be made to avoid movement of the neck, especially backward movement of the head, as when looking upward. In most cases, symptoms will begin to subside within 4 or 5 days. If symptoms persist unabated, medical consultation should be sought.

ACUTE DISC RUPTURE (CERVICAL)

Flexion-extension or rotational injuries to the cervical spine may cause tearing of the ligamentous structures that confine disc material to its intravertebral space. The disc material may herniate or "rupture" and compress the cervical nerve root as it exits the spinal canal to enter the arm. The result is a "pinched nerve" or cervical radiculopathy. Along with the neck pain, as described for acute neck strain, there is accompanying arm pain. The pain, ache, "pins-and-needles feeling" or "electric shock" often radiates from the shoulder to the elbow or to the fingers. Treatment is the same as for acute neck strain, taking special care not to extend the neck, that is, to bend the head backwards as to look up. However, if there are associated complaints, such as weakness or numbness in the arms or hands, weakness in the legs, or difficulty with urination, a physician should be seen immediately.

Back Injuries

ACUTE LUMBOSACRAL STRAIN

Sudden or excessive stress to the ligaments, tendons, and muscular elements of the lumbosacral spine can cause acute low back strain (lumbosacral strain or "lumbago"). Pain, "stiffness," or "tightness" is felt in the low back and often radiates to the buttocks and thighs. Pain is increased by standing or walking, and frequently the sufferer cannot straighten up from a bent-over position. Coughing or sneezing may aggravate the pain.

Treatment should begin with strict bedrest. Any comfortable position in bed is acceptable. However, most persons afflicted with acute low back strain find the supine (flat on the back) position with the hips and knees bent over one or two pillows most comfortable. The person should remain in bed until the pain subsides (4 to 5 days). Any activity requiring sitting or standing should be avoided. Visits to the bathroom can be minimized by using any convenient container. Eating in bed is not difficult when the patient is lying on his side. Muscle spasm and pain can be alleviated further by applying warm towels to the painful back and by taking small amounts of whiskey. Use of aspirin is helpful. If the pain subsides, activity may be resumed. However, those activities that stress the lumbosacral spine must be avoided. Sitting for long periods of time, lifting objects weighing more than 10 pounds, or excessive bending at the waist should be especially avoided for 10 to 14 days. If symptoms do not subside within 4 to 5 days, the person should be examined by a physician. Transportation to the medical facility can be quite uncomfortable, especially over rough roads. Lying in the back of a station wagon or back seat of an automobile is more comfortable than sitting.

SCIATICA

The injury that produced low back strain may damage the confining ligaments of the limbar disc, resulting in a herniated, or "slipped" disc. The disc fragment can compress the lumbar nerve root. Irritation of the nerve root produces radiating pain in the leg. The pain usually involves the back and outer aspect of the thigh, inner or outer aspect of the calf, or instep or heel of the foot. Initial management does not differ from the management of acute low back strain. Any associated leg weakness, especially the inability to pull back the foot or toes, or any difficulty in urinating may signal significant nerve root compression and necessitates immediate neurological evaluation by a physician.

Spinal Cord Injuries

Injuries of the neck, thorax, or back may traumatize the spinal cord. If the spinal cord is damaged, neurological function (muscle movement, sensation, bladder and bowel control) below the point of damage is disrupted completely or partially. Following damage to the upper spinal cord, the injured person will be unable to move legs or feet, will not feel a pin prick or pinch, will often dribble urine, and may demonstrate penile erection.

It is most important not to aggravate a spinal cord injury by injudicious movement. Every precaution should be taken to move the person as little as possible. If breathing is unobstructed and emergency care can be summoned, the victim should not be moved until emergency paramedics arrive. If the injury occurs in the wilderness, and safe transportation of the victim becomes the responsibility of companions, the following suggestions for care should be observed:

1. Move the victim as little as possible.

2. When movement is necessary, move the patient "like a log."

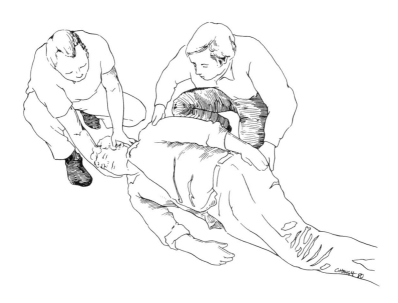

Log rolling technique

3. Always have one person hold the head steady and keep its position in relation to the body constant as the body is moved.

4. Prepare a hard, firm structure for transportation (wooden plank, automobile bench seat, boat oars secured together, etc.).

5. If the victim is lying on his belly, place the stretcher next to the person, then slowly "log-roll" the victim onto the stretcher. If possible, use as many as 5 people to roll the victim slowly so that no "buckling" of the neck and body occurs. Remember to have one person supporting the head and neck at all times.

6. If the victim is lying on his back, have 4 to 5 people slowly slip their arms under the person's back. At a given signal, the victim should be slowly lifted like a board and placed on the stretcher. Again, remember to support the neck and head.

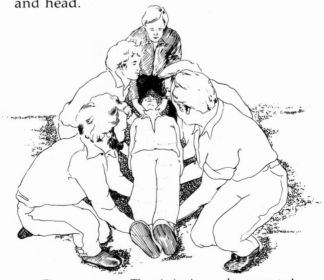

Five-man carry. The victim is evenly supported

7. Secure the patient to the stretcher and transport to the nearest hospital.

Peripheral Nerve Injuries

LACERATED NERVE

Any laceration of an extremity may partially or completely sever a peripheral nerve. After an extremity laceration, movement of muscles as well as sensitivity to pinprick beyond the level of the laceration should be checked. If any muscle weakness or significant sensory loss exists, medical consultation should be sought. A laceration should not be probed but simply covered with a clean dressing.

THE "FUNNY BONE"

The ulnar nerve traverses just beneath the skin where it passes in a groove of the humerus bone at the elbow. It may be traumatized during injuries to the elbow. Falls or a swinging flashlight or jackknife attached to the waist may directly contuse the ulnar nerve. The person experiences excruciating burning pain on the inner aspect of the forearm and hand as well as the little and ring fingers. The movement of the hand may be temporarily lost. The symptoms and signs usually last from a few minutes to a few hours. The injury is not serious and does not require immediate medical attention.

BRACHIAL PLEXUS

The brachial plexus is a sheath of nerves that arise from the cervical spinal cord, traverse the shoulder girdle, and enter the arm. This important collection of nerves may be damaged by sudden excessive side bending of the neck, forceful blows to the base of the neck and shoulder near the collarbone, or violent pulling of the arm from the shoulder joint. A person with such an injury may demonstrate paralysis or weakness of the arm, forearm, or hand. Numbness may be present also. Following such an injury to the brachial plexus, the arm should be immobilized in a sling and the victim transported to an emergency aid facility.

Obviously, there is not much that can be done in the field for many head and spine injuries, but careful observation, knowing what to look for, and knowledge of safe transport can make the difference between a possibly crippled or dead companion and a healthy hunting or fishing partner for next year's trip.

6

Emergency Eye Problems
in the Outdoors

The symptoms and signs of a problem with one or both eyes often create a dilemma for patients, friends, or partners. "Should I seek immediate medical attention?" "Can I wait until tomorrow or next week to see the ophthalmologist?" "Is there anything I can do now to keep the injured eye from becoming blind later on?" All of us have asked these questions before. Of all our senses, the one most precious to us is sight. Protection of your vision is of obvious importance. Let me introduce you to Joseph Olk, M.D., ophthalmologist and Fellow of Retinal Surgery at Washington University in St. Louis. Joe is a hunter and fisherman and as top notch a source of information as there is to tell you how to take care of your eyes outdoors.

Joe's purpose in this discussion is to acquaint you, the reader, with a framework of basic information regarding those eye problems most likely to be encountered outdoors, so that you may be better equipped to understand and handle initial care. It should be emphasized that this information is *not* meant to replace or avoid one's seeking medical attention.

External Anatomy

Prior to any discussion of eye problems it is necessary to define and illustrate the basic anatomical landmarks.

The eyeball itself has a thick outer shell composed of white fibrous tissue, called the *sclera*, and a central,

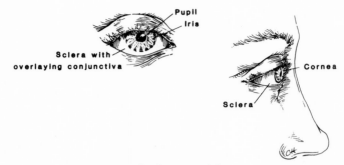

Front and side view of the eye

anterior transparent area, called the *cornea*, which is the "window" in front of the eyeball through which we see. The colored part of the eye, or *iris*, lies behind the cornea within the front segment of the eyeball. The central black hole in the iris is the *pupil*, a structure similar to the diaphragm of a camera, which opens and closes to control the amount of light that passes through. Overlying the sclera is a thin, almost transparent membrane, the *conjunctiva*, which contains many blood vessels. It is this membrane that becomes reddened and swollen when the eye is infected, irritated, or inflamed, and results in a red eye or "pink eye." The eyeball is surrounded by a bony orbit composed of seven bones, and these are covered with various protective layers, the outer layer being the eyelids with a row of eyelashes at each border. The lids and lashes serve as a protective cover for the eyeball, especially for the cornea.

Red Eye

This is perhaps the most common eye complaint, and many of the conditions causing a red eye are relatively benign disorders. The most common cause of conjunctivitis or "pink eye" is a virus, and the condition is like "having a cold in the eye." Also, certain bacteria and allergies can cause conjunctivitis, but these are less common. Whether of viral, bacterial, or allergic origin, most conjunctivitis is generally a self-limited process, lasting 3 to 5 days, and usually clears spontaneously without treatment. It is therefore important to attempt to differentiate conjunctivitis from those things causing a red eye that are potentially threatening and require *immediate* medical care. These conditions are keratitis (inflammation of the cornea); acute glaucoma (high pressure within the eyeball); and irritation or inflammation of the inner contents of the eyeball, called iritis or uveitis.

One can often differentiate conjunctivitis from other causes of red eye by the story alone. Persons with conjunctivitis will complain that the eye feels irritated, is teary, may itch, usually has a discharge with matter crusting on the eyelids, and may be associated with a recent head cold or fever. But if the person complains of blurred vision or loss of vision, pain, photophobia (sensitivity to light), or foreign-body sensation, this should steer you away from thinking of conjunctivitis. Sometimes people with conjunctivitis will have blurred vision due to mucous discharge, but this generally clears with blinking. Therefore, any person with these symptoms should not delay and should be seen by an ophthalmologist immediately.

Sudden Visual Loss

Most causes of sudden blindness are painless. Victims generally are unaware of the seriousness of this condition, yet it is important to recognize that this represents an ophthalmologic emergency, as early diagnosis and treatment might restore useful vision in many cases. All of the following are causes of sudden visual loss: vascular occlusions of the retina; acute glaucoma; hemorrhage; trauma; detached retina;

optic neuritis (inflammation of the optic nerve); hysteria; and certain poisonings.

While it is not the intent of this section to educate the reader in the differential diagnosis of sudden visual loss, the material here is meant to emphasize that sudden visual loss, even though usually painless, represents a true emergency and the affected individual should seek immediate attention from an ophthalmologist or family physician.

Trauma

Contusion injuries to the eye and orbit result from blunt trauma from a fist or foreign object. This can result in a fracture of the bones around the eye causing pain, swelling, and ecchymosis or "black eye." There may be numbness about the orbit and double vision. Blunt trauma to the globe of the eye may result in a rupture of the globe, hemorrhage in the eye, dislocation and disorganization of the contents within the eyeball, detached retina, or traumatic cataract. Immediate symptomatic relief can be obtained by cold compresses and analgesics, but in all cases, patients with blunt trauma to the eye or surrounding area should be evaluated by an ophthalmologist.

Lacerations of the eyelids can usually be repaired with adhesive strips, Steri-Strips, or sutures. However, if the laceration involves the eyelid margin, is deep in the upper lid, or involves the eyeball itself, immediate medical attention is mandatory.

Corneal abrasions result from either a foreign body or any object striking the surface of the cornea, resulting in a stripping away of the protective outer surface layer of cells. This usually causes pain, possible decreased vision, redness, and a sensation of "something" under the upper eyelid. A superficial foreign body may be irrigated off with sterile water or saline solution—a good one is Balanced Salt Irrigating Solution. Symptomatic relief can be obtained from covering the affected eye with an eye patch and taking oral analgesics for pain. If pain persists, or if the foreign body is embedded in the cornea, an ophthalmologist should see the patient. Any foreign body that penetrates the eyeball itself needs immediate medical attention. If you are unable to irrigate the foreign body off the cornea, *do not* attempt to remove it by any other means—just simply patch the eye and have the victim seen by a doctor. Don't play around; this is a classic example of the situation where you can do much more harm than good.

Chemical Injuries

Injuries involving acids or bases (lye) can result in very serious complications to the eyes. While nearly all chemicals are toxic to the eyes, the most potent damage is done by all basic solutions and chemicals, as well as hydrofluoric acid (HF) and concentrated sulfuric acid (H_2SO_4). These complications may be prevented or at least minimized by immediate and thorough irrigation with the nearest cool water or neutral solution available. If the victim is near a shower, place their head under it and irrigate continuously with the eyes open. If a sink or tub is available, fill it, submerge their head with the eyes open underwater, and move the head back and forth and from side to side to obtain a swirling-type action to irrigate the eyes. If near a lake, put the head underwater and repeat the same motions as described above. Continue irrigation or flushing of the eyes for at least 30 to 60 minutes. Remember, you cannot irrigate the eyes too long. If solid or particulate matter is in the eyes, be sure to evert the upper and lower lids and remove any particles with a cotton swab and then resume irrigation. In severe chemical injuries, irrigation may have to be continued for several hours. An ophthalmologist should be consulted in any case of chemical injury to the eyes.

Preventive Ophthalmology

While the previous discussion has centered on diagnosis and treatment of certain ophthalmologic problems, perhaps the most important and productive area of eye care is that of prevention. If you are aware of the potential dangers leading to blindness, hopefully you will take advantage of the opportunities for prevention by using sound judgment *before* the potential incident occurs.

This is a good place for us to talk about eyewear. If you wear glasses, you should have a backup pair. I, personally, have flipped a pair of glasses into Minn Lake in the boundary waters area when I tried to swat a wasp and got the glasses instead. If you wear contact lenses, bring a backup standard pair of glasses because even a minor eye irritation can make wearing contacts impossible. When you are walking through heavy brush or woods or when casting with two or more in a boat, safety glasses should be worn. Also, absolutely anyone with previous visual handicap in one eye should always wear safety glasses outdoors; there is no excuse not to when you could be one slip away from blindness.

A good pair of sunglasses is important for both summer and winter. Polarized sunglasses help even more because polarized glass intercepts and blocks reflected sunlight (glare), which can cause visual damage if exposure is prolonged, as with snowblindness or glare on water.

Infection in the eye may be very contagious and may be transmitted by touch, clothing, linens, etc.

Anyone having an eye infection should avoid touching the affected eye or the other, and use his/her own linens and towels. Also, any prescription or over-the-counter eye medication should be kept absolutely sterile and never used by anyone else. Old or unused medications should be safely discarded.

A complete routine eye examination by an ophthalmologist should be performed at least every two years, more often if previous problems have been diagnosed.

Again, Joe re-emphasizes, trauma to the eyes can be prevented by wearing properly fitted safety glasses or goggles. If you are in any situation where the possibility of eye trauma exists, wearing safety glasses or goggles may prevent a possible blinding disorder.

7

Emergencies Involving the Ear

The ear is an extremely complex organ made up of three main sections: (1) the external ear, (2) the middle ear space, and (3) the inner ear, containing the balance apparatus and the nerve for hearing. Otologic emergencies may involve any one of these three areas. Acute trauma and infection are most common in the external and middle ear areas, however.

Friends, Romans, and hunters and fishers, lend me your ears and I'll turn them over to one of the best in the business, Ruth Campanella, M.D. Ruth is an attending ear, nose, and throat surgeon at Rush-Presbyterian-St. Luke's Medical Center and an outdoor enthusiast. Ruth wrote the section on development of the ear for the *World Book Encyclopedia,* and now she has the facts to help you protect your hearing outdoors.

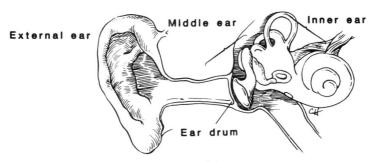

Cross-section of the ear

The external ear consists of the auricle, made of thin skin tightly bound to the underlying cartilage framework, and the external auditory canal, whose inner two-thirds is encased by the skull. The outer one-third has hairs and ceruminous glands, which produce earwax. The ear canal is S-shaped, to protect the middle ear from damage due to foreign bodies and debris. The eardrum separates the external ear from the middle ear space. This space is box-shaped and contains the three bones for hearing, which connect to the inner ear.

Sound enters the external auditory canal, setting the eardrum into motion. This vibration is transmitted to the bones that connect to the delicate inner ear nerve endings and on to higher brain centers where the sound is interpreted.

Emergency ear problems can be separated into two categories: Traumatic and infectious.

Traumatic	Infectious
Laceration	External otitis
Hematoma	Infected cysts
Thermal frostbite and burns	Furuncles
Eardrum perforation	Bullous myringitis
Barotitis	Suppurative otitis
Skull fracture	Chronic otitis
Foreign body	

When an ear emergency arises, two basic principles should be followed: (1) keep the area clean, and (2) avoid water. The least manipulation is the best policy to follow. Nothing should be placed in the ear canal, not even a cotton swab.

Traumatic Problems

Lacerations should be thoroughly cleaned, preferably with hydrogen peroxide or rubbing alcohol. The edges of the wound are then brought together with dry gauze and taped with Steri-Strips. If the cartilage is exposed, the skin edges are brought together over the cartilage and taped. Gauze or sterile cotton is then

molded around the ear and kept in place with a turban wrap head dressing. When the laceration is large
or the ear partially avulsed (torn off), the basic measures are followed and the victim should be taken to
the hospital immediately.

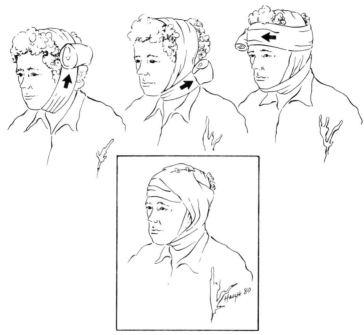

Full Head Wrap Technique

Hematomas (collection of blood) of the ear occur
following a blunt blow to the ear that results in bleeding between the cartilage framework and its overlying
skin. These accumulations of blood under the skin
look like big purple blisters. Treatment entails
removal of the blood clot and application of a con-
forming pressure dressing. Recurrent drainage may
be necessary to prevent the "cauliflower" boxer's ear
deformity, which will occur if the hematoma is untreated. The incidence of infection is high, and

knowledgeable medical advice should be sought immediately.

Frostbite is common in the exposed external ear. The ear is handled gently and should be allowed to thaw at room temperature slowly. No pressure-type dressings should be applied, to avoid additional tissue damage. Small blebs of fluid will appear but should be left intact. The dry dead skin will shed on its own. Extreme pain may occur during the thawing phase, requiring medication and hand restraints to prevent massaging the ears. Burns are handled in a similar manner. Cool soaks may ease the pain, but again, the blebs should be left intact to prevent infection and allowed to slough by themselves.

Traumatic eardrum perforations may occur from a penetrating object, an explosion, or slap with an open hand. The perforations usually will heal spontaneously without specific treatment other than strict avoidance of water in the ear. If the injury is accompanied by dizziness or facial paralysis, urgent medical consultation should be sought.

Barotitis involves a pressure sensation in the ear, decreased hearing, and pain. This follows barometric pressure changes associated with scuba diving and flying. Treatment requires oral decongestants, like Dristan or Contac, nasal spray, analgesics, and autoinflation of the middle ear space by chewing gum and yawning. Symptoms usually resolve in one to two weeks.

Any fall or direct blow to the head with or without loss of consciousness could cause a skull fracture. If a blue discoloration appears behind the ear (Battle's sign), bleeding occurs from the ear canal, or there is a loss of hearing, the victim should be kept at rest and medical attention sought immediately. It is important to note, as an observer or as a patient, whether the side of the face on which the blow occurred can be moved. Laceration of the facial nerve causes immediate paralysis and may require surgery. Delayed paralysis results from swelling of the nerve and often will disappear with observation only.

Foreign bodies in the ear should be left alone until appropriate medical expertise for removal is available. If an insect enters the ear canal, mineral oil can be placed in the canal to drown the insect while protecting the ear. The insect is then inert and can be removed at a later time. Impacted earwax should not be probed with a Q-Tip since the wax may be pushed further into the canal against the eardrum, producing pain.

Infections

External otitis, infection of the outer ear, is one of the more common infections involving the ear, especially after swimming. The ear is extremely painful, especially if it is handled. Lymph nodes in the region may swell and become tender. A discharge is present from the canal, and if swelling is severe, a hearing loss is noted. Treatment involves strict avoidance of water in the ear, local dry heat, analgesics, and antibiotic-steroid eardrops. If the condition develops in a diabetic patient, it requires urgent medical consultation to prevent extensive bony destruction and possible extension to the brain.

Infected cysts of the ear lobe or behind the ear often respond to local heat with spontaneous drainage. If the area becomes soft, the cyst may be opened and drained. This should be done in a sterile manner and the area kept meticulously clean after drainage. Boils in the ear canal are treated in the same manner, except that incision and drainage should be done by an ear specialist to prevent damage to the eardrum.

Bullous myringitis is a viral infection causing pain and complaints of a mild hearing loss. Blisters form in the ear canal and on the eardrum. Heat and pain medication relieve the symptoms, which recede when the blisters rupture.

Acute suppurative otitis media causes pain deep in the ear, fever, and decreased hearing. There is no discharge from the ear until the eardrum ruptures and the pain eases. Treatment requires systemic antibiotics for 7 to 10 days plus topical heat and analgesics, under direction of a physician.

Chronic otitis media involves a permanent perforation of the eardrum, which will become infected and drain if exposed to water. A person who has a known perforation must avoid swimming and keep water out of the ear while bathing. If a discharge begins, medical attention should be sought.

HEARING LOSS

Acute onset of a hearing loss in one ear is often due to early middle ear infection or impacted cerumen (earwax). Total hearing loss is often accompanied by loss of balance. The etiology is unknown, but a viral infection or a vascular blockage affecting the inner ear have been suspected as possible causes. The patient should seek medical advice immediately. Vertigo is loss of balance accompanied by a sensation of spinning and nausea, which is usually due to a viral inner ear infection if sudden in onset. An ear examination should be sought as soon as the patient can be transported.

Noise-induced hearing loss is a common side effect of repeated gun blasts or a large explosion. A permanent high-frequency hearing loss plus a decrease in the ability to understand what is heard is due to the damage produced by the sound on the inner ear nerve. All people are susceptible to this damage. If a decrease in hearing is noted immediately after exposure to a loud noise, this could be a temporary threshold shift, and hearing should return to normal in 2 to 4 hours. Earplugs or headphones should be worn at all times by people exposed to such noises, especially shooters.

Adequate hearing protection is a real must, especially for those of us who are exposed to repeated loud explosions—skeet shooters, trap shooters, all rifle and pistol bench shooters, and absolutely anyone shooting indoors. This repeated pounding to the ears will definitely cause hearing loss to some degree (sometimes severe) if the ears are not protected. If you think headphones interfere with shooting, at least get a good set of earplugs—and use them; they won't do any good in your pocket.

The ear is delicate, and the least possible manipulation after trauma or infection is the best course of action. Avoidance of water and cleanliness will often suffice during the initial emergency treatment. Medical examination should not be delayed for an extensive period of time if pain persists. Ruth reminds you that any signs of lethargy or decreased consciousness requires emergency trained medical evaluation.

8

Dental Problems Outdoors

It had happened twice in the past two weeks, and it was happening again now. The tooth that had bothered Jack before was starting to ache again for no reason. Jack was loading the Blazer to leave on a fishing trip he had been planning for six months, and he wasn't about to let a little ache in a tooth stop him. And it didn't stop him until he and Les and Alex were in northern Minnesota on Sunday morning, still six hours from the fishing lodge. They had to waste all of Sunday's daylight trying to find a dentist for Jack. No one was very happy—especially Jack. One very nice, and, I might add, a somewhat expensive trip, was ruined by a toothache.

Our wisdom on teeth comes from Richard Wren, D.D.S., a hunter and fisherman, past assistant professor of Dentistry at the University of Illinois and University of Chicago, and now in private practice in Chicago. Let's listen to what Dick has to tell us about how to avoid dental problems outdoors.

The most important message, as you can see from the story of Jack, is that if you spend $400 to $1,000 once or twice a year to go hunting or fishing, it certainly is worth spending an additional $50 to $100 a year to go to see a dentist to make sure that your teeth are as healthy as possible so that an unfortunate toothache doesn't step in and wreck a perfectly good trip.

In dentistry, as well as in most areas of medicine, prevention is the name of the game. Seeing a dentist and making him aware of the situation that you're going to be in—hunting or fishing out in an area

where there is no readily accessible health care support—is one of the best things that you can do to make
your trips enjoyable and to prevent something from
wrecking them. While it is true that not all situations
are preventable and that some things may occur that
cannot be foreseen, it is also true that having a dental
checkup a month before you go on a fishing trip will
prevent your teeth from ruining a trip that is very
important to you.

We will deal here with several things that can
occur while you are fishing. They generally break
down into two major areas—dental emergencies (by
that I mean tooth emergencies) and traumatic injuries. In most cases dental emergencies are preventable;
traumatic injuries are not as preventable, but we will
deal with them and try to give you an idea of what
you can do to help yourself or a companion when you
are on that fishing trip away from immediate help.

DENTAL EMERGENCIES

The first area we shall deal with is tooth pain; second, tooth fractures, and third, swelling and/or abscess formation.

There are certain signs that can make you aware
that a tooth may be going to cause you trouble. The
first of these signs is spontaneous pain. Any tooth that
begins to ache or to have pain for no apparent reason
is a tooth that you should be worried about. Something is wrong—in the tooth, in the nerve of the tooth,
or in the gums that surround the tooth. The second
sign is a reaction of a tooth to hot, cold, sweet, or
sour—a reaction that lasts a long time, that is. Sometimes teeth will be sensitive, especially to hot and cold,
but when the stimulus is removed, the pain goes away
immediately. This reaction is merely a defense reaction on the part of the tooth; however, if a tooth is

sensitive to the stimuli and the pain persists for 15 to 20 minutes or longer, then there is something to be worried about concerning that tooth. The third sign is sensitivity to biting pressure. If a tooth is sensitive when you bite down on it, or when you are chewing your food, then this tooth has a potential to cause problems. You should specifically ask your dentist to look at teeth with these problems and try to find out what is causing the pain.

If, you are on a fishing or hunting trip and a tooth begins to ache and hurt you, what can you do about it? Generally speaking, the only adequate remedy while you're on the trip is to take some form of analgesic to control the pain. Second, you can try to avoid the stimuli that caused the tooth to ache. If it reacts to cold or hot, then moderate the temperatures. If it is sensitive to sweet and sour, try to avoid foods that have these qualities. Third, try to avoid chewing on that side of your mouth, as much as possible. The analgesics that you can take generally are aspirins, Empirin, or Tylenol. However, it might be wise to take with you a stronger analgesic that you could get on prescription from your dentist, such as Empirin with codeine or Tylenol with codeine. Carry that in your emergency kit so that if you have a problem, you'll have a stronger analgesic to control the pain.

The second area to deal with is tooth fractures. The most likely sign that teeth may fracture are very large silver fillings, or large anterior fillings. When more than 50 to 75 percent of the tooth structure is made up of filling material, the walls of the tooth become weakened to the point where they are prone to fracture. If undue force, in eating or sometimes in clenching your teeth, is put on the tooth, it may fracture the cusps or the tooth structure that remains. Very often the best thing to do to prevent this is to have these teeth crowned so that the tooth is literally surrounded with gold and given strength to prevent these fractures.

What do you do if a tooth fractures while you are on a trip? The first thing to do is to have a friend look in your mouth and check the tooth. With a pair of large tweezers or cotton forceps, have your friend remove any small loose pieces or any pieces of filling material that are loose. This will prevent your swallowing or aspirating (going down the windpipe) these pieces accidentally. Then, you can deal with the tooth. If the tooth is only mildly sensitive to hot and cold or to air blowing on it, or, if when you avoid these stimuli, it is not sensitive, then generally you can wait until you're finished with the trip to go and see your dentist. If, however, the tooth aches continually, take some cotton, and moisten it very lightly with oil of cloves. Dry it thoroughly and place the cotton pellet over the site or over the area of the ache. This will usually sedate the pulp and prevent it from aching further. Also, you can take analgesics, as was advised in the first section on tooth pain.

Third, we will deal with swelling and/or abscess formation. If you have a swelling around the gums of a tooth or in the gum tissue and it is localized through a relatively small area, it is generally being caused by some food or other debris that has become lodged under the gums. This can usually be taken care of by placing your toothbrush bristles at a 45-degree angle to the gum tissue, and massaging the area under the gum with bristles, using a very short stroke, so that debris is removed. Or, you can take a toothpick, and very gently place the toothpick between the teeth, to try to remove whatever debris is in there. After removing the debris, thoroughly rinse your mouth and especially the area of the swelling with an appropriate mouthwash, such as Cepacol, or Listerine. If, however, the swelling or the abscess formation is generalized and involves more than just the margin or the edge of the gum tissue or is located in the posterior section of any arch and you still have your third molar teeth (your wisdom teeth); or if the swelling is located in the jaw and causes a swelling of the outside of the face, then you should immediately consult your nearest local hospital or dental or oral surgeon's office and have the area looked at. Swellings or abscesses of this type can grow very quickly and can be very dangerous. Usually, if they are generalized and large, they will be accompanied by a fever. Again, the treatment for large swellings is to seek immediate professional help.

One last problem that should be mentioned is canker sores in your mouth. If canker sores develop while you are on a trip, they can be very annoying and uncomfortable. The best remedy for them, while on a trip, is to take a cotton swab, dip it in a bottle of Camphophenic, and gently dab the Camphophenic over the canker sore, which is usually located in the soft tissue of the mouth. In doing this, you will eliminate, for the most part, the pain caused by the ulceration of the soft tissue, and will control most of the discomfort of the canker sore.

TRAUMATIC INJURIES

The second major area to be dealt with is traumatic injuries. These are injuries caused by a fall, or by a blow, or by something hitting the teeth or the jaws. In the case of fractured teeth, what must be determined is the extent and the seriousness of the fracture. If a tooth has a relatively minor fracture, it can be treated as we have already advised. If, however, the entire crown is fractured from the tooth or the tooth is fractured vertically, then different problems are presented. If an entire crown is fractured off and the tooth is very sensitive, oil of cloves, as previously mentioned, will usually control the pain, together with analgesics. If the tooth is fractured vertically, then whether or not it is painful will determine your action. If it is not painful and presents no serious problem and there are no loose fragments, then you can wait until you get home to see your dentist. If, however, there are loose fragments on a vertically fractured tooth, or if you begin to have pain in the bone around the tooth, then you should seek professional help immediately and have that tooth removed.

Sometimes a tooth is knocked loose and moved out of its normal alignment. The most important thing to do here is, with your fingers, to move the tooth back into its normal position so that you can bite down and not interfere with it. Then seek professional help immediately to have the tooth splinted so that it can heal.

Sometimes a tooth is avulsed, or knocked completely out of its socket in one piece. If a tooth is knocked completely out of its socket and is found, it should be thoroughly washed off with cotton and clean, clear water.

Wash off the root section, and then immediately take the tooth and replace it in the tooth socket. Very often it will be difficult to place it all the way in the socket. Sometimes this can be relieved by slowly pumping the tooth up and down in the socket and removing some of the blood there. Once the tooth has been placed in the socket and lined up into its normal position, you may bite down on it carefully and then seek immediate help to have the tooth splinted. It is important here to emphasize that, once a tooth is moved back into position or placed back in a socket, it should be splinted that day if at all possible to secure it in place. A really loose tooth could be aspirated (go down the windpipe) while sleeping, and this could lead to serious infection in the lung. Aspirated teeth must always be removed as soon as possible, so please be very careful. If reaching a dentist that same day is impossible, it is probably safer to leave the tooth out and wrap it in the cleanest possible cloth soaked in mild salt water (approximately 1 teaspoon of salt per quart of water), and get to a dentist as soon as possible.

The last two areas — fractured segments of the bony housing of the teeth and fractured jaws — will require professional help as quickly as it can be obtained. However, there are things that you can do to stabilize the area while you seek professional help. The signs of fractured alveolus or fractured jaws are when you look in the mouth and see sharp deviations in the alignment of teeth. Generally, some sections of the teeth will be higher or lower than others, and the teeth will not bite normally. For example one tooth is high, and the very next tooth is appreciably lower. In these cases, very gently take the section that is misaligned and slowly move it back into alignment, if this does not cause too much pain. If the alveolus or bony housing is fractured, once it is placed in alignment, the person can bite down gently and hold the teeth together, and this will serve to splint the teeth and maintain the alignment; a bandage can then be wrapped around the lower border of the chin and jaw up over the top of the head to keep the teeth together and maintain the alignment. Likewise with a fractured jaw, one of the injured person's partners or friends can gently take the two sections that are in misalignment and slowly move them as much as possible and realign them so that the teeth are even, unless this is too painful. Once this is done, the injured person should then bite down on the area gently, hold it in place, then place a bandage around the lower jaw and tie it over the top of the head to maintain the teeth in their proper alignment. If this is very painful, just stabilize the jaw and get to professional help as soon as possible. If the injured person wears dentures, it is more difficult to see the fractures. If they can be seen, the soft tissue should be aligned if possible; then the patient's dentures should be placed in the mouth. The mouth should be closed gently so that the teeth are together, and the emergency bandage placed around the lower jaw up to the top of the head. Very often it may also be advisable to tie a bandage gently around the front of the lower chin and the back of the neck. In this way, the segments will be stabilized both vertically and horizontally until you can get to a hospital or dental office to have more definitive stabilization of the segments done.

Finally, let's go over what you should have in your emergency kit for a dental emergency. First some analgesics. These should include both aspirin and/or Empirin and some Tylenol tablets. Generally, 3 or 4 packets of either is satisfactory. Second, you may also want to have a few tablets of Empirin with Codeine or Tylenol with codeine, one-half grain, to control the more serious pains and toothaches until help can be reached. These can be obtained on prescription from your dentist. Third, you should have a pair of long tweezers or forceps, along with some cotton, some cotton swabs, a bottle of oil of cloves, and a small bottle of Camphophenic. Have a good trip!

9

When the Problem Is the Airway

When we talk about the upper airway, we mean the path that air takes from the nose or mouth through the larynx (voice box) to get to the windpipe and lungs. Trouble in breathing is the most serious and most frightening result of injury to this area. It is frightening because it occurs rapidly, with little warning, and goes on to deprive vital tissues of the body, such as the brain and heart, of the oxygen needed to survive. When all breathing stops, irreversible damage to the brain will occur after only 4 minutes. As a first priority, therefore, you must establish a way to breathe quickly and effectively. In this chapter we will discuss airway problems and what you can do in the wilderness to turn a potential disaster with possible fatal consequences into a manageable problem.

Talking to us on airway problems is Dino Delicata, M.D., formerly of the Department of Otolaryngology and Bronchoesophagology of Rush-Presbyterian-St. Luke's Medical Center, now in private practice. Dino is a hunter and fisherman who knows well the forests and streams of Maine, New Hampshire, and Vermont where he grew up. Dino, like so many of us who hunt and fish, also enjoys cooking wild game and makes a real mean stuffed brook trout. Unfortunately, he didn't include that recipe in this chapter, but it *is* stuffed with lots of good things for sportsmen to know about airway problems outdoors.

First, let's talk about the problems that are not too serious but can be irritating to the camper or outdoor enthusiast who does not know how to manage them.

The nose is an important channel for the passage of

air. The air we breathe in through the nasal airway arrives at the lungs filtered of irritating particles that might otherwise be harmful. In infants, it is important to remember that, unlike adults, they can breathe only through their noses. They develop the ability to mouth breathe only after several months, therefore, it is wise to keep mucus and debris out of their one and only airway. The nose can perform these valuable functions because its lining is very sensitive and richly supplied by blood vessels. This protective function is enhanced by the sense of smell, which not only gives great pleasure, as with the fragrance of bacon cooking on a crisp fall morning, but also warns us that we should not be breathing in fumes that could injure our lungs.

A nosebleed can occur from a variety of causes, most commonly dry air. The dry air produced by hunting lodges and cabin stoves will parch the delicate mucous membranes of the nose, and these tissues will crack and bleed, just as chapped lips do. A deformed nose bleeds more easily than a normal nose, but anyone may get a nosebleed, especially after a night's sleep in a dry, warm room.

Remember that all types of bleeding, not just bleeding in the nose, will respond to pressure if that pressure can be directed to the site of bleeding. Don't bother applying cold rags to the back of the neck, throwing your head back, or using other home remedies. Simply pinch the soft part of the nose together forcefully (if it doesn't hurt, you're not doing it hard enough) and hold it for 15 minutes by the clock. This action will stop 95% of all nosebleeds. If pinching doesn't work and bleeding is severe, go to the nearest emergency facility, since prolonged uncontrolled blood loss may be severe enough to require blood transfusion. Nosebleeds not controlled by pinching should be seen by a doctor, who will probably pack the nose with vaseline-coated gauze. This packing provides more direct and effective pres- 'sure to the bleeding site. About 1% of the people do not respond to this treatment and must be hospi- talized. If you injure your nose by a sharp blow or fall, it may also bleed. Just as with a fracture in any other part of the body, a broken nose will swell, especially over the bridge, and may look bruised. Treat the nosebleed first, just as we have already mentioned. In addition, if the bridge of the nose is swollen and bruised, apply cold compresses as soon as possible. Soak a clean handkerchief or face cloth in the coldest water available—ice water is preferred—and apply to the nose. Keep a compress on the nose for 20 minutes each hour for the first 24 to 28 hours. Cold helps the small blood vessels that are torn and bleeding under the skin to stop bleeding, will diminish the amount of swelling and discoloration that would normally occur, and should relieve pain quickly and without medicine. *Do not use dry ice.*

Injury to the inside of the mouth or to the jaw is potentially dangerous. Swelling in this area can obstruct the oral airway and may progress rapidly to make breathing through the mouth impossible. When the injury is severe, get to a hospital or base station as soon as possible. If, however, the injured person already has trouble breathing, you can help by grab- bing the tip of the tongue with cloth-wrapped fingers and pulling the tongue forcefully forward. This sim- ple action may rapidly re-establish the oral airway until you can get to medical help. If the tongue is bleeding, apply pressure by squeezing it firmly be- tween your fingers. Try not to touch the back of the tongue, the part furthest back in the mouth, as this will cause the injured person to gag. The gag reflex may lead to vomiting and lung injury if air passages are filled with stomach acid and food. This can be a very serious complication.

When should you suspect that a swollen, bruised jaw may be broken? To test for this, simply have the person bite down hard on a pencil or twig. Pain will be felt immediately in the area of the fracture or break. If this is the only injury, cold compresses to that area will once again help to decrease the swelling. The patient should avoid chewing solid foods until a physician can further evaluate the injury. If the skin is torn, wash with an antiseptic soap and apply a dressing, as clean as possible, over the area of injury to keep dirt out of the wound.

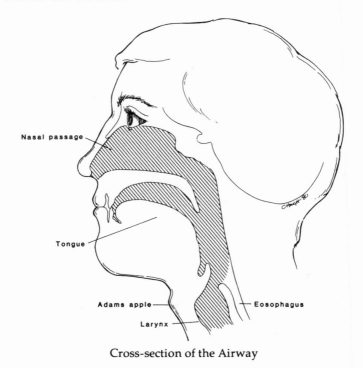

Nasal passage

Tongue

Adams apple

Larynx

Eosophagus

Cross-section of the Airway

The voice box, or human larynx, is a structure that

you can see in the neck, especially in males. We commonly call this the "Adam's apple." This cartilaginous or bony framework houses the vocal cords and resembles the prow of a ship. A sharp blow to the neck can fracture the larynx, especially in older individuals, whose voice boxes are more brittle. This injury is extremely serious. Danger signs include swelling over the larynx and either hoarseness or total voice loss. The neck may look black and blue. The most important problem, however, is difficulty breathing. If you notice any breathing problems, don't wait! Get medical help as soon as possible. The larynx guards the airway to the lungs, and a little swelling here can be rapidly fatal without much warning. During transport, keep the injured person sitting upright, as still as possible, and don't let the victim talk. These three actions will open the remaining airway and help prevent inhalation of blood, often found in the throat after such an accident. If by some chance you have oxygen available, use it, and let the valve run wide open. You must then move quickly to the nearest emergency medical aid.

When you are dealing with a larynx fracture, don't try any heroics, such as an emergency tracheostomy. Forget about trying to jab a pen or penknife in anyone's neck unless you have been specifically trained in where and how to establish a surgical emergency airway. You will probably cause permanent damage, pain, and bleeding, and most important, you will not improve the situation for the injured person. The conservative approach will deliver the patient safely to help in a far greater proportion of cases than heroics will.

"The cafe' coronary", the airway obstructed by food, is the next subject. While sitting around the fire with good friends, after a day's hunting, a sportsper-

son has had a "Few too many". This alcoholic over-
dose numbs the mouth, throat, and vocal cords. The
same numbing effect that makes alcohol a good pain
reliever has now set the stage for "the cafe' coronary."
The victim swallows a large piece of meat or poorly-
chewed food quickly or carelessly and it suddenly
"goes down the wrong pipe." Instead of traveling
down the esophagus to the stomach, the lump of food
lodges in the larynx. This irritation normally makes a
person cough violently as a reflex, pushing the food
out of the airway and back into the mouth. The alco-
hol-anesthetized individual, however, will have a
diminished gag and cough reflex. Suddenly the person will become blue, unable to talk, and will struggle
for breath, which cannot go in or out. Death can
ensue if the airway is not rapidly reestablished. Do *not*
slap the person on the back. If you have ever tried fix-
ing an axehead or hammerhead onto a handle by
striking the end of the handle on the ground, you
know what happens. The hammerhead goes down the
shaft and lodges firmly onto the handle. The same
situation exists when the victim is hit on the back,
wedging the lump of food more tightly into the larynx
or moving it further into the windpipe. Do not turn
the person upside down, either. This will not help,
except to terrify an already frightened person. The
situation can be managed effectively by remembering
exactly what has happened. The person has both
lungs full of air trapped behind a plug of food jammed
just at or below the vocal cords, which are usually in
spasm, meaning that the cords can neither open nor
close effectively. Now, if you remember the way a
popgun works, you can use the same idea. Pistonlike
force suddenly increases the pressure in the gun bar-
rel behind the plug or cork in a popgun, popping it
loose from the position in which it is lodged. You can

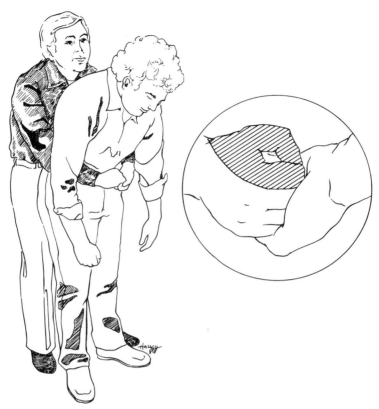

The Heimlich maneuver. Enlargement shows locked
hands. Shaded area indicates area of hand used for thrust

use this technique without changing your victim's
position. If the person is upright or seated, employ
what is referred to as the Heimlich hug or the Heimlich maneuver. Stand behind the victim, and lock
your arms in front of him or her, around the waist,
with your hands locked together. With the victim's
back braced firmly against your chest, pull your
hands sharply towards you in an upward motion to
the rib cage in one continuous movement. It is important that the maneuver be done as quickly as possible
so that the movement of the hands is a jolt or thrust.

This pistonlike effort will push the contents of the abdomen against the diaphragm and instantly empty both lungs of air, popping the obstruction loose. Immediately the person should begin to breathe again. Sweep your finger across the back of the mouth to clear the ingested material out. If the victim is on the ground or floor, place him or her on the back, seat yourself astride the thighs, and place both hands together flat on the belly with the heel of your hand at about the level of the belly button. Next, press down as deeply as you can and deliver a sharp, continuous push up and toward the rib cage. Again clear the mouth. If the patient is not breathing, begin mouth-to-mouth breathing and cardiopulmonary resuscitation until independent breathing begins.

Finally, if you have any doubt about the seriousness of an injury sustained, especially to the larynx, in an area where time is a significant factor in arrival to the nearest trained medical personnel, do not treat. Better to be guilty of being too cautious than to risk the life of a friend.

10

Chest and Abdominal Injuries

Chest and abdominal injuries are potentially lethal, regardless of where they occur. But outdoors, away from immediate medical aid, the outdoorsperson who does not recognize or appreciate the seriousness of such injuries or their immediate management is at a great disadvantage. There are obviously only a few things that can be done in the field for serious chest or abdominal injuries, but knowing those few things can make the difference between survival or death for you or your friend.

Advising us on chest and abdominal injuries is Alex Doolas, M.D. Alex is a general surgeon whose special areas of interest are cancer and trauma surgery at Rush-Presbyterian-St. Luke's Medical Center in Chicago. Alex is also Professor of Surgery at Rush Medical College. He is an avid hunter and fisherman, whose special love is waterfowling. We have shared many excellent days of duck and goose hunting together, but today I'll shoot out of the next blind down the line so you can join Alex. While you wait for the mallards to come in, you can listen to what he has to say about chest and abdominal injuries.

In general, chest and abdominal injuries are classified as penetrating or nonpenetrating. The penetrating injuries are easy to diagnose, since there will be a wound entering the body. Nonpenetrating injuries are usually a consequence of vehicular accidents, falls, or blows that leave no obvious external evidence of injury, and, therefore, the presence or absence of an internal injury is not obvious. For this reason, any nonpenetrating or blunt injury of severe

enough nature to produce pain must be considered a
serious one and the victim medically evaluated.

Anatomy of the Chest

The chest cavity is protected by ribs and muscles
and is divided into right and left sides by the
mediastinum. The mediastinum contains the heart
and the great vessels that course to and from the
heart. It also contains the windpipe, called the trachea, which carries air to the lungs, and the
esophagus, which connects the mouth to the stomach.
The lungs are large air sacs interlaced with numerous
blood vessels carrying oxygen to the heart and from
the heart to the entire body. The atmospheric pressure
in the chest cavity is somewhat less than that of the
atmosphere, and because of this difference, the lungs
are kept expanded. In general, penetrating injuries to

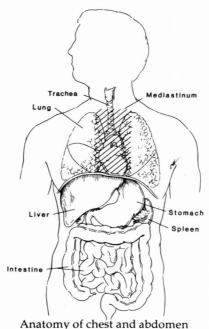

Anatomy of chest and abdomen

the heart and great blood vessels will cause rapid, massive bleeding.

Chest Injuries

Injuries to the chest can be superficial or deep. Superficial injuries are those that involve only the skin and muscle of the chest wall. It is often very difficult to determine whether the injuries are superficial or deep. Therefore, they must all be taken seriously and the injured person should be evacuated to a medical facility. Bleeding should be stopped with a compression bandage after the wound is cleansed with germicidal soap. Attempts at probing the wound or trying to remove lodged foreign objects should be avoided. If foreign objects such as arrows or pieces of wood are lodged in place, they must not be removed lest further injury be produced by their removal; fatal bleeding might ensue if the foreign object has dammed up a bleeding point. The shaft of the arrow or piece of wood can be cut off to avoid difficulties or further trauma in transport to a medical facility. Forget about the old movies—leave the arrow where it is—got it? Good!

Fractures of the ribs can be caused by a fall, and they can readily be recognized by extreme pain upon breathing in, or pressure on the involved rib. A simple rib fracture can be best treated by a compression bandage to splint the rib and prevent further pain during transport. The victim must be evacuated because fractures of the ribs may signify injury of deeper structures, such as the spleen if the rib fracture is low on the left side, or the liver, on the right side. The broken ends of fractured ribs may puncture the lungs or the heart. A lung puncture can result in a collapse of the lung, pneumothorax, massive bleeding, infection, and pneumonia.

PNEUMOTHORAX

A pneumothorax occurs when there is air within the chest cavity and around the lung. When the lung is punctured or a hole or opening is created in the chest wall, the decreased pressure within the chest rises to atmospheric pressure so that the pressure inside and outside the lung are the same. When the pressure difference needed to keep the lung inflated is gone, the lung collapses, as do the small air sacs that get oxygen into the blood, and the victim feels short of breath. Sometimes a puncture of the lung will also create bleeding, and the victim may cough up blood.

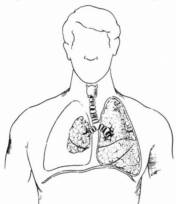

Diagram of Pneumothorax

Evacuation to a medical facility must be started immediately, but the first thing to do in the case of a penetrating chest wound is to check to see if it is a sucking chest wound. A sucking chest wound allows air to get into the chest cavity as the patient breathes in, but when the patient exhales, the air cannot get out because the hole is blocked by the lung or other tissues. More and more pressure develops within the chest cavity, eventually compressing the uninjured lung and preventing normal blood return to the heart. If this process continues, death will occur. Recogni-

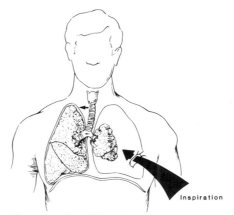

Diagram of sucking chest wound

tion of a sucking chest wound is done by listening near the chest wound for the hissing sound of air being drawn into the chest. Treatment is to seal the wound. This can be done by pressing the palm flat against the wound until an airtight bandage can be made. Many things will work as an emergency airtight seal—a piece of rubber raingear, Vaseline gauze, plastic wrap, or even the cellophane from a cigarette pack can be used with a tight bandage to seal a sucking chest wound. The victim should be turned onto and kept on the injured side; this will take some pressure off of the uninjured lung and heart and increase chances of survival. The victim must be transported to a medical facility with all possible speed.

HEMOTHORAX

In most penetrating chest wounds, there will be a degree of blood in the chest cavity; this is called *hemothorax*. The presence of blood and air in the chest cavity is called *hemopneumothorax*. Hemothorax can be caused by bleeding from the lung or the blood vessels themselves or from a puncture of the heart or great blood vessels. This is very difficult to recognize in the field and must be expected in every penetrating chest wound. Treatment is application of dressing to prevent a tension pneumothorax, placing the patient on the injured side to allow the good lung to function, and rapid evacuation to a medical facility.

Subcutaneous emphysema is the collection of air underneath the skin. This is caused by escape of air from the lung or trachea in penetrating injuries. Often this is very extensive, covering the neck, chest, and body. Subcutaneous emphysema feels to the touch like cornflakes in a plastic bag. Whenever this feeling is present, a pneumothorax has probably occurred; evacuate the patient rapidly to a medical facility.

FLAIL CHEST

When an individual sustains a massive blunt injury to the chest, numerous fractures of the ribs may result in an unstable chest. The patient is unable to breathe adequately on that side, and therefore air cannot be exchanged even in the good lung. A large bulky dressing must be placed over the unstable chest and the chest taped tightly to prevent to-and-fro movement. Any accompanying sucking chest wound must also be treated; the patient must be placed on the injured side and rapidly evacuated

Injuries to the mediastinum and/or the central part of the chest are potentially very dangerous due to bleeding from the heart or great blood vessels. Any penetrating injury that seems to have gone near the mediastinum or through the chest must be a signal for a rapid and safe evacuation of the individual.

Anatomy of the Abdomen

The abdomen is separated from the chest by the diaphragm, which is a muscle affecting respiration by moving up and down, much like a great bellows. The abdomen contains the solid organs such as the liver on the upper right part of the abdomen and the spleen in the upper left side of the abdomen. The kidneys are in the back part of the abdomen, and the rest of the abdominal cavity contains the stomach, the intestines, and the colon. The middle and back portion of the abdominal cavity is occupied by the major blood vessels, the aorta and the vena cava, which carry blood to and from the lower body.

The lowermost and front aspect of the abdominal cavity is occupied by the urinary bladder. Disruptive injuries to the hollow organs such as the stomach and the intestine will cause peritonitis within 8 hours of the time of injury, and injuries to the solid organs such as liver, spleen, and kidneys will cause bleeding.

Injuries to the Abdomen

Just as with chest wounds, abdominal injuries are penetrating or nonpenetrating. Most penetrating injuries due to bullet wounds will go through the abdominal wall and injure the abdominal contents. Knife wounds, on the other hand, will injure the abdominal contents only half the time, according to statistics. Despite this fact, it is very difficult to determine whether a knife wound has penetrated the abdominal wall or not. For this reason, any person with *any* penetrating wound of the abdominal wall should immediately be taken to medical help.

Any deep penetrating injury to the abdominal wall will cause marked pain. Wounds that pass through the abdominal wall and enter the abdominal cavity will create pain of an increasing degree until there is extreme tenderness to any movement or pressure, signifying full-blown peritonitis, which is infection of the cavity lining. Penetrating abdominal wounds should be covered with a sterile bandage and soaked with germicidal solution such as Betadine. The patient should be made as comfortable as possible and should be given absolutely nothing to eat or drink.

A victim who is given anything to eat or drink will probably vomit and may even add to the spread of infection within the abdominal cavity. The victim will also complain of dryness of the mouth and thirst because of reflex action of the injury. Any ingestion of water, however, will cause vomiting and further dehydration. If anything, just moisten the victim's mouth and lips with a damp cloth. There should be *absolutely* no attempt at probing the wound to see the extent of the injury, and no lodged foreign body should be removed.

In the case of shotgun injuries with large destruction of the abdominal wall and protruding organs, the organs must not be pushed back into the abdominal cavity because of the danger of further contamination. The organs should be covered with a clean, moist germicide soaked bandage and the victim carefully evacuated to the nearest medical aid. I really don't have to add "as quickly as possible," do I? OK, *as quickly as possible.*

Blunt injuries to the abdomen often result in bleeding from a ruptured spleen, liver, or kidney, and therefore the victim must be placed at rest, must not be given water or food, and must be rapidly evacuated.

Because of the dangerous nature of most abdominal and chest injuries, the safest mode of action is evacuation of these patients unless the injuries obviously are superficial and the patient's pain subsides rapidly.

11

The Sportsperson and Chronic Disease

Many people enjoy hunting, fishing, and other outdoor activities. In some of them, however, a chronic condition such as asthma, diabetes, epilepsy, or heart disease may develop during their lifetime. This need not keep them from continued participation in outdoor activities as long as proper planning precedes their outings. This planning involves knowledge of the disease and the disease process by both the outdoorsperson and his or her companions. This knowledge should help all parties prepare adequately for the trip, and anticipate any problems that may arise.

Although, in this chapter, you are made aware of possible problems and the preventive measures that should be taken, this chapter is in no way meant to be a substitute for professional medical advice and treatment. It's a good bet that if you have a chronic illness, the advice that follows, which comes from Mark Round, M.D., could be lifesaving. Mark is a specialist in internal medicine and an avid outdoorsman. I hope that, rather than discouraging people with chronic illness from fishing, hunting, and camping, Mark's advice will encourage them to—with the proper planning—enjoy, even more, the pastimes that mean so much to them.

The following is a general list of "musts" for a person with a chronic ailment who is considering an outdoor adventure.

1. Wear a medical alert bracelet including
   a) Medical diagnosis
   b) Allergies

2. Carry a medical information card including
    a) Name
    b) Address
    c) Personal physician's name and phone number
3. Carry a list of all medications
4. Know the location of the nearest hospital
5. Inform companions about all possible problems related to the disease and appropriate solutions
6. Have well-equipped first-aid kit including
    a) Germicidal soap
    b) Topical antibacterial ointment
    c) Sterile bandages
7. Have an ample supply of medication
    a) In a pillbox on their person with label identifying each medication according to use and dose
    b) In the tent in cool, dry place
8. Discuss the details of the proposed trip with their personal physician before beginning the trip.

Now we will discuss the individual disease entities and their particular problems and preventive measures.

Asthma

The first chronic disease for discussion involves the respiratory tract. It is commonly known as asthma or bronchial asthma. Approximately 9 million Americans suffer from bronchial asthma. Asthmatic attacks occur when there is a spasm of the tubes that carry air into the lungs. The spasm causes victims to feel tightness in the chest and wheezing. Along with the sneezing, the patient will experience shortness of breath. The severity of the symptoms varies from attack to attack.

A number of important facts should be remembered about asthmatic attacks. The attacks are often started by inhalants like pollens, molds, and animal dander, all of which a sportsperson is likely to contact in the field. Also, cold and exercise will increase the spasm of the lung passages. Cold exposure can be properly prevented by dressing appropriately. This includes the wearing of a face mask when out in the cold. Face masks are available at most pharmacies.

Exercise tolerance varies from one asthmatic to another. Some asthmatics cannot tolerate continuous, vigorous exercise. These people should consult their physicians concerning the advisability of a hunting trip before they make plans to go. Other asthmatics can tolerate continuous physical activity. These people should undergo physical training at home before they venture into the field on a trip requiring vigorous, prolonged physical activity. Physical activity should always be preceded by a warm-up period.

The spasm of lung passages in asthma may be marked, and it may be relieved either spontaneously or with treatment. The treatment can be continuous or intermittent (for acute attacks). Some asthmatics receive continuous medication. This medication is generally in the form of pills or inhaler.

Prior to making a trip into the field, the asthmatic should check the supply of medications. An adequate amount of medication should be taken on the trip. The asthmatic and all traveling companions should know the location of the hospital that is closest to their camp in case of an emergency.

Most asthmatics are very knowledgeable about their disease and understand what to do for an acute attack. Sometimes the medication a patient has for the acute attack is not adequate to relieve the spasm of lung passages and the shortness of breath. In that case, it is the job of the companion to transport the asthmatic to the nearest hospital at once. The hospital emergency room will provide the patient with treatment that will relieve the spasm and shortness of breath. Quite often the patient may go home once improvement occurs.

Diabetes

Diabetes mellitus is commonly called just "diabetes," and it affects about 10,000,000 Americans. It is a very complex disease that requires proper management by a physician. Patients with diabetes may require special diets, pills, or insulin injections. Once a diabetic is under the care of a physician and has the proper dosage of medication worked out, he or she may live a fairly normal life, which may include outdoor activities like hunting and fishing.

Diabetic people, including those who take insulin, are fairly knowledgeable about their disease. They know when to adjust the insulin dose, when to ingest sugar, and when to call their physician for assistance.

The diabetic person must remember several facts when planning a trip. First, the person should plan for the same good control of the disease that he or she has when at home. This includes eating properly, taking good care of the body, and taking medications as is done normally. Menus for the trip should be planned ahead of time.

Preparation for the trip should also include packing appropriate clothing. Clothing should protect the arms, legs, and feet from possible injury. Therefore, the appropriate dress includes long-sleeved shirts and slacks. Shoes should always be worn by diabetics when outdoors. In addition, an adequate supply of the patient's medications should be packed for the trip.

Provision should be made so that the medications (especially insulin) can be stored in a cool, dry place during the trip. The location of a nearby hospital should be known by the diabetic and all companions. Another important addition to a safe trip is a well-equipped first-aid kit, including germicidal soap, antibiotic ointment, and abundant sterile dressings, to clean, coat, and cover any cuts or abrasions.

Some diabetic persons have complicated treatment programs. These programs include testing of urine for sugar and acetone. This testing should be maintained during all trips.

Diabetic persons receiving insulin injections as part of their treatment are subject to a number of problems. These problems involve abnormalities of blood sugar level. As stated above, the diabetic is very knowledgeable about the disease and can generally tell from the testing that is done or from symptoms when abnormalities of blood sugar occur and make moderate adjustments in insulin or diet to compensate. These symptoms that occur with abnormal blood sugar are listed as reminders to you.

> *High blood sugar:* weakness, thirst, dry mouth, urinary frequency, nausea, vomiting, abdominal tenderness, rapid breathing, and acetone breath (chemical or fruity smell to breath)

> *Low blood sugar:* headache, hunger, shaking, sweating, blurred vision, weakness, nervousness, decreased thinking ability.

If the symptoms are mild, the diabetic can treat himself or herself. Mild symptoms of low blood sugar can be treated by eating sugar or hard candy. High blood sugar requires diet, fluid, and insulin treatment. If these symptoms are marked, it is the duty of the diabetic's companion to transport the diabetic to the hospital as soon as possible. Coma (an unconscious state) may occur with either high or low blood sugar. A diabetic patient in coma *must be taken to the hospital for emergency care!*

The diabetic on insulin should discuss outdoor activity with the physician before making a trip. The trip will most likely involve an alteration in the diabetic's usual amount of activity, since exercise has the same effect as insulin. This alteration will require that the physician make changes in the insulin dose and/or diet.

Many injuries are possible during the course of an outdoor adventure. Even minor injuries may become serious to a diabetic if proper care is not taken. Diabetics tend to heal poorly. Their injuries must be vigorously treated to prevent serious infections. Treatment of injuries is discussed elsewhere in this book. The injuries should always be evaluated by a physician as soon as possible.

Epilepsy

Epilepsy is a chronic disease that is poorly understood by the general public. Epilepsy has several causes but commonly occurs after violent head trauma. A patient with epilepsy is subject to seizures.

Seizures are also called "convulsions" or sometimes "fits" (slang). They are due to an abnormal increased electrical discharge of brain cells. This electrical discharge occurs simultaneously in affected brain cells. The form of the seizure depends on the number of brain cells involved, the location of these cells within the brain, and the direction of spread of the electrical activity from these cells.

The epileptic patient is generally taking one or more medicines for the prevention of seizures. When planning a trip, the epileptic should make sure to take along an ample supply of medications. The epileptic patient should *never* skip taking medications. The epileptic should also make traveling companions aware of the disease.

The epileptic should discuss with the physician the amount of activity permitted. Obviously, someone who is still having frequent seizures should not be allowed to ride horseback, go climbing, or engage in other dangerous activity. An epileptic who is well controlled on medications should be able to engage in vigorous physicial activity provided that recurrent head trauma is avoided.

Certain things can cause more frequent seizures. These things include drug abuse, alcohol abuse, and a lack of sleep—all of which should be avoided by the epileptic, whether at home or on a trip in the wilderness.

Seizures may be very frightening to those who have never observed them. The most frightening to the observer is the grand mal seizure. To promote better understanding, a brief discussion of the events involved in a grand mal seizure follows.

The epileptic first collapses, the body stiffens, and breathing stops. During this period of 2 to 20 seconds, the patient turns blue and the jaws clamp shut. The second stage is a short period of jerking movements when saliva foams in the mouth. During the jerking period, the epileptic loses bladder control and urinates involuntarily. After this period, the epileptic is tired and confused and usually sleeps for several hours.

During a seizure, the epileptic's companion has several duties to perform. The epileptic should be aided to the ground. A pillow or blanket should be placed under the epileptic's head to prevent trauma during the seizure. When the jaws clamp down, the tongue may be bitten. If possible, this should be prevented by placing a wrapped tongue depressor or padded stick in the mouth. Once the jaw is clamped shut, it should not be forced open. Forced opening of the jaw might cause more damage than is already done. After jerking stops, place the head lower than the body, turn the head to the side, and hyperextend the neck. Hyperextension of the neck may be accomplished by putting one hand under the back of the neck and raising it while pushing down on the forehead (see Figure 11-2). This maneuver enables the epileptic to breathe by opening up the airway.

Hyperextension of the neck

The important thing to remember about seizures is that repeated seizures may be dangerous. If a second seizure occurs without the epileptic regaining consciousness between the two, then the epileptic must be taken to a hospital immediately for emergency care.

Heart Diseases

Heart disease is a common problem in the United States. Many people suffer from various types of heart disease. Some of these people lead fairly normal lives. It is this group of individuals who might enjoy a sporting adventure.

Many heart patients have special diets and medications. Planning diets and obtaining an adequate supply of medications for the trip are essential preparations. In addition, the trip should be discussed in detail with the patient's physician.

Many problems can occur with people who suffer from heart disease. The most common of these problems are irregularities in heart rhythm, angina pectoris, and heart attack.

Irregularities in heart rhythm can cause the heart to stop its pumping action. This will lead to death within minutes. Use of cardiopulmonary resuscitation (CPR) when the heart stops pumping is likely to save lives. CPR training is available through most local branches of the American Red Cross and/or Heart Association. (See the chapter in this book on Cardiopulmonary Respiration).

Angina pectoris is chest pain due to shortage of adequate oxygen in the heart tissue. Angina occurs upon exertion and is relieved by rest. People who occasionally suffer from angina may be able to tolerate the exercise required for some sporting activities. When angina pectoris occurs, the patient may have shortness of breath and sweat a great deal. After the person has rested for less than 15 minutes, the pain of angina should disappear.

A chest pain that lasts longer than 15 minutes is a

danger signal. The person suffering from that pain should be taken to a hospital immediately.

Summary

Sporting activities and the outdoors may be enjoyable to people who suffer from chronic diseases. These people, with their special problems, require extra preparations for their outdoor adventures. Occasionally these people must take extra precautions or must partially restrict their activities. An outdoor adventure can prove safe and worthwhile provided that the chronically ill person follows the simple suggestions in this chapter.

12

The Outdoorsperson and Infectious Diseases

The outdoorsperson is ever broadening his or her spectrum of activities and is, thus, placed in environments considerably different from the surroundings at home. He or she may come in contact with potentially harmful, and even fatal, infectious diseases involving bacteria, viruses, protozoans, ticks, worms, and other life forms. The purpose of this article is to review some of these areas of concern and to inform the adventurer of what should and should not be done. Some of the best advice on critters much too small to see but capable of causing big trouble for us outdoors comes from Gary Trager, M.D., of the Section of Infectious Diseases at the University of Illinois College of Medicine. Gary's favorite times are spent cross-country skiing and camping, so let's join him at his campfire, sip a cup of hot coffee, and hear about some of God's smallest and deadliest creatures.

Diarrhea is one of mankind's most common ailments, and there are many types of infectious gastrointestinal illnesses that might affect an outdoorsperson. One of the more frequent causes is that due to toxins produced by bacteria growing in food. The most widely known kind of toxin-produced food poisoning is "staph" food poisoning caused by the various *Staphylococcus* species. These organisms grow and produce their toxins in food that is slowly cooling after cooking or left unrefrigerated on warm days. Within 1 to 6 hours after the eating of toxin-containing food, vomiting and abdominal pain develop. These symptoms usually last only 4 to 8 hours and rarely longer than one day. Fever is not present, and the only therapy required is control of the vomiting (over-the-counter preparations are generally effective) and intake of fluids to prevent dehydration. The most important preventive measures are promptly refrigerating all foods not intended for immediate consumption and not allowing people with skin infections to prepare meals (since *Staphylococcus* may also reside in diseased skin).

Another toxin-produced food poisoning is due to *Clostridium perfringens*, the same bacterium that causes gas gangrene. When a contaminated meat or poultry dish is cooked at less than 100°C (water boils at 100°C and temperatures at or over 100°C kill the organism) and is then allowed to cool, *Clostridium perfringens* will grow and make its toxin. This food (such as a meat pie) when eaten, may produce an illness in 8 to 12 hours characterized by abdominal pain and nonbloody diarrhea, but no fever. Antidiarrheal agents such as Pepto-Bismol or those containing kaolin are usually effective treatment although the disease rarely lasts more than one day. As in staphylococcal food poisoning, prevention is best accomplished by eating meat well cooked and hot or after adequate refrigeration at 5° C.

Another type of food poisoning is caused by a bacterium *(Vibrio parahaemolyticus)* found in raw fish and shellfish along the Atlantic, Pacific, and Gulf coasts of North America. Within 12 to 24 hours after eating contaminated seafood, nausea, vomiting, abdominal pain, and diarrhea develop, which may be accompanied by fever and chills. The illness lasts only a few days, and the measures mentioned earlier will be helpful, although for severely ill patients antibiotics are available. Thorough cooking of fish and shellfish is effective in preventing the disease and is preferrable to treating the disease once is has been established.

Typhoid fever is caused by the bacterium *Salmonella typhosa* but is associated with person-to-person transmission. Other Salmonella infections, however, can be passed from animals to humans. The largest reservoirs of the disease are domestic fowl, turkeys, and ducks (including their eggs). The probability of infection is lessened but not totally eliminated by cooking the meat or eggs. Water contaminated by the feces of infected fowl may also cause the illness. After ingestion, the organisms grow in the intestine and, within a day or two, fever, abdominal pain, and diarrhea appear. The stools may even contain mucus or blood. Although this malady will usually resolve within a week, it can be prolonged. A more severe case, with the spread of infection throughout the body may occur at times. The mainstay of treatment in the usual case is relief of the diarrhea and a liberal fluid intake. Antibiotics generally are not required. Cooking of fowl may not render it noninfectious, but it does significantly reduce the chance of *Salmonella* infections.

Giardiasis is also an intestinal infection caused by the amoebalike protozoan *Giardia lamblia*. Mild infections frequently pass unnoticed, while more serious infestations may cause nausea, abdominal cramps, and loose stools. Giardiasis is contracted by drinking infected water, which is especially common in certain areas of New York State and the mountain zones of Colorado. Municipal water treatment plants adequately remove the organism. Therefore, drinking from lakes and streams presents the greatest risk of infection. Giardiasis can usually be readily diagnosed and treated by most physicians, particularly if they are aware of where the patient has traveled. The best plan, however, is to not drink untreated water.

A true amoeba, *Entamoba histolytica,* causes the disease amebiasis by the ingestion of its cysts in contaminated food (especially fresh vegetables) or water. This organism can be found worldwide, but particularly where sanitation is poor. The cysts become active in the intestines, and most infections are without any symptoms. When symptoms do occur, however, they include diarrhea and abdominal cramps. The diarrhea may persist for weeks and be associated with weight loss, low-grade fever, and blood in the stools. Examination of the stools and a blood test are helpful in making the diagnosis. Several possible antibiotics are available to treat this disease but, unfortunately, there are no effective preventive steps at this time.

For intestinal infections in general, any illness that persists beyond two or three days and is associated with fever or blood in the stools or is present in an entire group of travelers should best be cared for by a physician. This will avoid prolonged debility and help prevent potential epidemics.

Most people are aware that any break in the skin may be the starting point for tetanus, commonly referred to as "lockjaw." What they don't know is that this disease is actually caused by a poison made by the bacterium *Clostridium tetani* that has been introduced into the wound and allowed to grow. This organism is amazingly common and is found in the soil and in fresh and salt waters. When symptoms appear, the initial wound may have already healed. The involuntary spasms and contractures of the body's muscles are the most prominent features of this illness and have led to the name "lockjaw"; they may cause death by interfering with breathing. Physicians are able to treat tetanus, but stopping it before it starts is more important and much easier. Make sure your tetanus shots are up to date. This can be achieved by full immunization with three doses of toxoid given at 4-week intervals, followed by booster doses every 5 to 10 years and by ensuring that any wounds, bites, etc. encountered are properly cleansed and treated.

Once the scourge of humankind, plague, caused by the bacterium *yersinia pestis*, still occurs throughout the world. In North America, it's found westward from the Rocky Mountains. This infection is transmitted to many by the bite of an infected flea. These fleas are carried by ground squirrels, prairie dogs, chipmunks, deer mice, rabbits, and hares. The location of the bite usually goes unnoticed, but within a week fever develops with weakness, and painful swelling of the neighboring lymph glands. If untreated, the victim will become too weak to stand, and go into shock, and this carries a high mortality rate. Specific and effective therapy is available but is of little benefit if not started early in the illness. All contacts of the patient require close observation for signs of the disease and, at times, may need precautionary antibiotics themselves. There is a vaccine for people at high risk of contact with possibly infective fleas; however, the best way to reduce plague is effective flea control programs and repellants. Be careful when you're skinning animals.

Brucellosis is an infectious disease of mammals that can also infect humans. It is caused by several species of *Brucella* organisms, which are found in ill horses, mules, caribou, deer, moose, and hares in addition to domestic cattle, swine, sheep, and kennel-bred dogs. These organisms are found throughout the infected animal and remain alive for three weeks even in refrigerated carcasses but are killed by cooking, smoking, curing, and the pasteurization of milk. *Brucella* may invade humans through the eyes, nose, intestine, genital tract, and broken skin. Symptoms begin within a few days to several months after exposure. These manifestations include fever, weakness, sweats, chills, and generalized body aches and are in no way distinctive. This means that the patient needs to inform the physician of any contacts with animals so that the physician can order the appropriate diagnostic tests. Many infections may appear to cure themselves within 6 months, but the symptoms may recur without further exposure. Antibiotic therapy is both safe and effective. Domestic animals can be examined for the presence of this infection through a blood test, but this obviously can't be done to wildlife. A vaccine can afford some protection to persons with frequent animal contact, but wearing gloves when handling animals is something everyone can do to reduce the risk of brucellosis.

Tularemia is a hazard to hunters, campers, trappers, sheep herders, and mink and muskrat farmers. It's caused by the bacterium *Pasteurella tularensis*, which may parasitize over one hundred different mammals. Rodents, and, particularly rabbits are the main sources of disease. Handling of infected carcasses may result in the introduction of the organism into the skin, which will lead to fever and a large ulcer at the site. Another form of tularemia can result from small amounts of airborne organisms created when animals are being disemboweled. These organisms may then be inhaled and result in bronchitis or an unusually severe, and possibly fatal, case of pneumonia with fever, chills, cough, chest pain, and shortness of breath. Again, be especially careful when cleaning and skinning animals. Diagnosis of this disease is not always easy, even by the most expert physician. Thus, the person's occupational and recreational history is critical to proper treatment, since specific antibiotics can be used in treatment. Avoidance of the illness by handling all wild rodents with rubber gloves is to be encouraged. A vaccine is available for forest rangers and similar persons whose pastimes place them in daily contact with potentially infective animals.

Rat-bite fever is also related to rodents such as mice, rats, weasels, and squirrels. It is caused by the bacterium *Streptobacillus moniliformis*, which resides in the animals' mouths. About a week after a bite, the disease begins with fever, chills, and headache, even though the bite wound is healing nicely. This is followed by a generalized rash and painful, swollen joints. The physician requires knowledge of the victim's habits and vacations to consider the possibility of this illness and begin the appropriate diagnostic and therapeutic maneuvers. Prevention is possible only by the obviously good practice of avoiding animal bites. But, if you are bitten, see your doctor, promptly.

Leptospirosis is a bacterial disease that we can catch by contact with environments contaminated by the urine of infected rodents, pigs, cattle, and horses. Thus, fish cleaners, animal handlers, and those who swim in infected waters are risking this disease. These organisms can't penetrate healthy skin, but any scraped or diseased skin renders a person susceptible. The incubation period is 1 to 2 weeks, although some infections may be totally silent. Fever, chills, headache, weakness, red eyes, swollen glands, and a rash can occur and, in severe cases, pneumonia, meningitis, kidney failure, and yellow jaundice may be present. Treatment is available, but in the severe form of leptospirosis (Weil's disease) deaths still occur. Control of the host animals and purification of the environment is not practical, but a vaccine can be obtained for people who are at high risk for the disease.

Fear of rabies is centuries old and well founded because of virtually certain death for anyone who acquires this infection. Rabies is a virus that is found worldwide in wildlife, the main source of the disease in North America. In early 1979, however, there was a canine outbreak at the Texas-Mexico border. The major carrier animals are foxes, skunks, livestock, and vampire bats. This illness is transmitted by a bite that implants saliva containing the virus near nerve tissue. The virus then migrates to the nerve tissue. Saliva deposited on intact skin or on a scabbed-over cut however, is not infectious. The virus then travels through the nerves to the central nervous system (brain and spinal cord). Because of this, the closer the bite is to the head, the more dangerous the situation is. The disease begins with fever, headache, and nausea, associated with tingling at the bite wound. This progresses to severe neurologic abnormalities with foaming at the mouth and is followed by total collapse. Since there is no specific thereapy and survivors are few and far between, prevention is of the greatest importance. Wounds must be thoroughly cleaned and medical care sought immediately to determine whether vaccine and/or antiserum are needed. People who are at great risk of contact with rabid animals (wildlife control officers and spelunkers) may receive periodic vaccinations to raise their immunity to this dread disease. Exposure to caves with many bats can lead to rabies infections, even though there was no direct contact with the animal, and medical care should be sought in these instances as well.

Mosquitoes may cause illnesses in humans aside from the hives that usually result from their bites. They may transmit certain viruses which can cause meningitis or other serious neurologic diseases. The viruses are originally from birds or small mammals that are infected and have been a source of a blood meal for the mosquito. Because there is no specific therapy and no vaccine, abatement of the mosquitoes by comprehensive programs is the only means of control. Of course, individuals can minimize exposed areas of skin by wearing long pants and shirts and should apply mosquito repellents to those areas still exposed.

Most outdoors people are familiar with Rocky Mountain spotted fever (RMSF) and know that it's transmitted by certain types of ticks (especially the Rocky Mountain Wood Tick and the American dog tick) when they take a blood meal. The disease may be found anywhere in North America, but the majority of cases occur in the Carolinas and Virginia. The main features of RMSF include headache, fever, muscle aches, mental confusion, and a rash that starts on the hands and feet and quickly spreads to the trunk. If this disease is suspected, and there is a history of a tick bite, medical care must be sought immediately because RMSF may end fatally if not appropriately treated. Personal measures to reduce the chances of a tick bite include applying repellents to the exposed skin areas and visual inspection of oneself and one's companions several times each day for ticks. Once attached, a tick can be removed in several ways, particularly if something hot such as a match or heated knife blade is touched to it. It should never be squeezed or crushed, as this may actually increase the chance of transmission of RMSF.

Another disease related to ticks is Colorado tick fever, which is found not only in Colorado but in the entire western United States from April through July. It is caused by a virus passed on through the bite of an infected tick. About 4 or 5 days after a bite, fever and chills begin with muscle aches and red eyes. This subsides in 2 or 3 days, and, in about 50 percent of the victims, is followed in another few days by a similar bout. There is no therapy needed except rest, fluids, and pain relief, since there is essentially complete and total recovery.

Tick paralysis is caused by the same ticks that cause RMSF—the Rocky Mountain wood tick and the American dog tick. A poison secreted by the tick enters humans only after the tick has been attached and feeding for at least 1 day. Onset of the illness is heralded by restlessness, tingling in the head and extremities, and is followed by difficulty in walking and standing. It may progress to total paralysis resulting in death from respiratory failure. Unless the paralysis is advanced, a complete recovery can be achieved within a day or two of simply removing the tick in the manner mentioned earlier. The victim's hair must be examined closely for ticks hiding there. There is no specific therapy, so people venturing out should take the same precautions described to prevent RMSF.

There are three kinds of tapeworm infestations that one might encounter on hunting or fishing trips. The first is the beef tapeworm *(Taenia siginata)*, which may cause an itchy sensation in the rectal area, abdominal pain, and nausea. Passage of pieces of the tapeworm in the stool, however, is the most common symptom of the disease. This worm is transmitted to humans by the eating of raw or partially cooked beef. Treatment is safe and effective, but prevention of the infestation can be easily achieved by thoroughly cooking all beef. Another tapeworm, the fish tapeworm *(Diphyllobothrium latum)*, is found in such freshwater fish as pike, salmon, trout, turbot, and whitefish around Alaska and the Great Lakes regions. Infection of this worm usually produces no symptoms at all, but an anemia, similar to pernicious anemia, may develop. Diagnosis is readily made by a stool examination, and treatment is identical to that used for the beef tapeworm. Freezing, thorough cooking, drying, or pickling fish will ensure the prevention of any illness, and eating raw, or partially cooked fish should be discouraged. The third tapeworm is *Taenia solium,* the pork tapeworm. This tapeworm is more dangerous than the other two. The disease is transmitted by eating raw or minimally cooked pork. In Mexico, as many as one out of every fifty swine is infected, and thus the disease can become widespread. Usually, the symptoms are similar to the illness produced by the beef tapeworm, but a severe form of the disease (cysticercosis) with seizures and damage to the nervous system, may result. The milder infestation is easily diagnosed and treated, but cycticercosis frequently requires hospitalization and various potent medications. Cooking pork until the pink color is gone is the best assurance of not becoming infected.

There are two roundworms, or nematodes, that humans may encounter either in the city or in the country by coming in contact with soil in which the larvae live. These two worms are *Necator americanus* (hookworm) and *Strongyloides stercoralis.* These worms live almost everywhere but are most frequently found in tropical and subtropical climates. They enter humans by penetrating the skin of the foot, and cause local discomfort and a rash, called ground itch. They may then spread throughout the body to cause pneumonia, abdominal cramps, nausea, and vomiting. Again, treatment is available if the disease is established, but prevention by avoiding the wearing of sandals and by not going barefoot is preferred.

Another nematode with which outdoorspeople should be acquainted is *Trichinella spiralis,* the causative agent of trichinosis. These worms may be found in the muscles of practically any flesh-eating mammal, but wild and domestic swine are the major culprits. Even bear meat has been known to be infected. When infected meat is eaten, the worms become adults in the intestine and produce a myriad of larvae. These larvae then migrate to the muscles, where they may cause pain, swelling, and weakness, although mild cases will have no symptoms at all. Most people recover totally without any therapy a few weeks after the illness begins, but for those who are not quite as fortunate, there are medications available. Trichinosis is best prevented by only eating meat that has been adequately cooked (as for tapeworm prevention), frozen or salted and dried for a long period of time.

Hirudiniasis is the medical term for the attachment of leeches to the skin. They are commonly found in or near lakes, ponds, and streams. As is well known, they suck blood and frequently do it painlessly. The person usually becomes aware of leeches by finding them adhering to an exposed arm or leg. The only treatment required is careful removal of the leech followed by a thorough cleansing and bandaging of the wound to prevent secondary infection. The actual removal of a leech needs to be done in certain ways so as not to leave any mouth parts in the bite wound. Pulling the leech off is not recommended. Touching the leech with a lighted match, a hot knife blade, or vinegar is effective. Chemical repellents applied to the skin are helpful, and boiling all drinking water will prevent the swallowing of a live leech, which may cause severe internal disease.

There are several types of flukes that cause

schistosomiasis, but, in the Western hemisphere, only *Schistosoma mansoni* is of importance. It is confined to freshwater areas of Puerto Rico and Lesser Antilles. After a complex relationship with certain snails, the free-swimming larvae may penetrate the intact skin of swimmers or waders. This causes a local rash and, at times, fever, headache, and muscle aches. These organisms then find their way into the veins surrounding the intestine, where they mature to adults and lay eggs. This can be associated with abdominal pain, weight loss, diarrhea, and the accumulation of fluid in the abdominal cavity. Cirrhosis of the liver may be a late complication and result in death. Because the eggs are passed in the patient's feces, the diagnosis can be made by examining the stools. However, most physicians will not consider this illness unless the patient mentions travels to locations where the fluke is encountered. Therapy is available when this fluke is found to be the cause of disease, but there is no vaccine. Control of schistosomiasis through its intermediate snail host is an ongoing program. Travelers to infected areas are best warned about the dangers of swimming or wading in fresh water. Again, avoiding the disease is the best and easiest medical advice.

Sporotrichosis, caused by the fungus *Sprorothrix schenkii*, is a disease that we contract from plants. This fungus grows in soil and on decaying plant life and is introduced to man through a puncture of the skin (as from the thorns of a barberry bush). A nodule, or lump at times with some ulceration, appears at the puncture site, followed by similar nodules along the course of the draining lymph glands. Those nodules may drain thick material but cause little pain. This illness can frequently be diagnosed just by looking at the lesions, especially if the physician is aware of a patient's contact with thorns or needles. Oral medications will virtually always cure this fungal disease, but wearing gloves while working outdoors to avoid the infection is far more beneficial.

A summary of the infectious diseases that an outdoorsman might encounter has been presented by Gary in this chapter. There are, however, many more illnesses that have been associated with the animal kingdom, especially mosquitoes (such as malaria) that are not a problem in North America. For the traveler going to the more exotic areas of the globe, a call or visit to the local Department of Public Health will supply the information needed to make the adventure safe and full of fond memories. By following the simple suggestions mentioned in this article, the outdoorsperson should be able to go anywhere or do anything and avoid potential infectious diseases. If an animal is killed or found, and its skin, meat, or organs are the least bit suspicious for illness, the animal requires careful handling and should be destroyed to prevent the spread of disease to humans or other animals.

13

Chemical and Food Poisoning in the Outdoors

The term *food poisoning* describes a state in which the victim suffers an acute attack of abdominal pain and diarrhea, sometimes accompanied by vomiting and usually lasting 1 to 2 days, but on occasion a week or more. The onset is usually sudden and may commence as early as 2 hours or up to 40 or more hours after eating the contaminated food.

No one wants to give up any time on an outing, much less be incapacitated for a week or more from something that, with a little care, can be avoided. Most of the hints that follow are just common-sense ways of avoiding food poisoning. Hopefully, they will serve as a guide for new campers and perhaps reminders for those of you who are more experienced. Here's some good advice from the old camp cook himself, Tom Suttie, R.Ph. Tom is a research pharmacist with the Rush-Presbyterian-St. Luke's Poison Control Center, and the only thing he enjoys more than wilderness canoe trips—he's traversed over 300 rapids of the Colorado River—is camp cooking. Take your plate and fork over to the campfire and help yourself to a serving of some plain talk about food, water, and camp sanitation.

"Obviously, safe food will not cause food poisoning," Tom says. What causes a food to be harmful has filled volumes. This includes such things as high levels of toxic metals such as zinc, copper, or antimony; the food itself may be poisonous or, as is usually the case, the food may be infested with toxic living organisms. These organisms are invisible except when

129

viewed through a microscope. Their presence in food may be demonstrated whether by food poisoning symptoms when food looks, smells, and tastes normal, or by spoilage, when it looks, tastes, and smells bad.

Certain foods will not allow growth of food-poisoning organisms, for example, acid foods such as sauces, pickles, and some soft drinks. Foods with a high sugar content—jams, syrups, and honey—and foods with a high fat content discourage growth of bacteria, although the bacteria may survive. In dried or frozen foods organisms cannot multiply, but a proportion of those already present before freezing or dehydration will live on.

Water

The most important thing to all outdoorspeople is pure water. Any of us can generally get along a while longer without a drink, just moistening our lips with water. But if one drop is contaminated, it can so sicken us that, if nothing worse, we'll become too weak to travel. Assume all water is impure unless recently proved otherwise by a laboratory test.

If natives drink the water without ill effects, they may have developed a certain degree of immunity to tainted water. The same water could make a newcomer quite uncomfortable. High mountain streams may be quick-running and look and smell pure, but upstream a few yards may be the decaying carcass of an animal. The safest principle, wherever you are, is to assume all water is impure.

The next problem is how to purify the water. Boiling will rid water of germs. How long to boil usually depends on the altitude and contaminants. Generally, 5 minutes is a safe time. As a general rule, when a campsite is set up, the first thing that should be put on the fire is a large kettle of water to be used in cooking and washing utensils. All water that enters the human body should be purified. That includes water in which a toothbrush is dipped, water in which food utensils are washed, and water used in cooking. Boiling water *will not* remove industrial pollutants or pesticides. Also, just to complicate things, some viruses are resistant to short periods of boiling.

Because the air has been driven from it, boiled water tastes flat. The air and the taste can be restored by pouring cooled water back and forth between two clean jars or by shaking it in a partially filled jar. Some even add a pinch of salt. Care should be taken when adding salt to water, because too much will give the water a cathartic property.

The next best method of water purification is by means of chemicals. Those used are halazone tablets, chloride of lime powder, tincture of iodine, and iodine tablets.

Two halazone pills will ordinarily make a quart of water safe in a half hour. If the water is really questionable, double the amount of halazone and the time. Halazone will have little effect on viruses, however.

Chloride of lime should be used in the following manner:

1. Dissolve a heaping tablespoon of chloride of lime in 8 quarts of water. (2 gallons)

2. Add one part of this solution to 100 parts of water to be disinfected.

3. Mix, and wait at least 30 minutes before using.

In an emergency, tincture of iodine from the first-aid kit can be used to purify water. Place 1 drop in 1 quart of water, mix, and wait about 30 minutes. To be extra safe, double the amount and the time.

Iodine water purification tablets contain tetra-glycine hydroperiodide and have been adopted as a standard for the armed services. They are used as follows:

1. Add one tablet to a quart of water in a container with a cap.

2. Wait 3 minutes.

3. Shake water thoroughly, allowing a little to leak out and disinfect the screw threads before tightening the cap.

4. Wait 10 minutes before drinking or adding beverage powders; if water is cold, wait 20 minutes.

5. If water contains decaying vegetation or is murky or discolored, use two tablets for every quart.

6. Make certain that the iodine disinfects any part of the container that will come in contact with the drinker's lips.

Another good thing to remember is that the addition of liquor or ice to water may add flavor, but it does not rid water of germs. In fact, ice may be a source of contamination.

Foods

Most food poisoning occurs from the mishandling of fresh foods or unsanitary conditions. This does not mean that campers must suffer a monotonous diet of beef jerky and beans. With the new advances in freeze drying, the variety and abundance of the diet can be almost as great as the imagination of the cook.

However, never take more than one meal (the first night's) of fresh meat unless you have a means of refrigeration. This holds true for milk and other dairy products such as cheese. Fresh eggs can be taken and if wrapped individually and well packed, will last, even in hot weather, for more than a week. However, the new varieties of freeeze-dried eggs are so close to the taste of fresh eggs that this added care in packing and bulk required is probably not warranted.

Freeze-dried foods, while generally less apt to cause food poisoning still leave something to be desired in the way of taste and aroma. Following are a few tips on how to liven up your diet.

Bacon, if purchased in slab form and heavily smoked, will last up to 3 weeks. The sliced type will spoil in 2 to 3 days in warm weather.

Butter packaged in plastic bags and placed in aluminum or tin containers will keep from 7 to 10 days. Margarine may keep a bit longer. It may possibly be kept longer if the container is placed nightly in a cool stream or lake.

Cheese is generally not suggested for long trips, but some sharp cheese in slab form will last up to a week, and grated cheese packed in plastic bottles will last a little longer. Grated cheese helps make freeze-dried spaghetti, vegetable dishes, and eggs or omelets a real treat.

Don't forget that with spices there is no spoilage to worry about, and they can make or break camp cooking.

Honey, jam, or peanut butter are all filling and high in energy content. They are great for lunch or trail snacks when spread on leftover flapjacks or on some sort of cracker.

On your next trip try leaving all the Kool-Aid type mixes at home. Instead, try fruit juice crystals that are not merely flavoring like Kool-Aid, but are derived from the actual fruit. One packet makes a quart of juice. It is not necessary to make the drink full strength. Sometimes just a few crystals dissolved in your canteen or cup will remove the Halazone taint.

Finally, try to plan all the meals so the food is well cooked and eaten hot and there are no leftovers. Avoid allowing food to sit in the open and cool before eating, and don't reheat or use leftovers. This will eliminate many of the camper's food poisoning problems.

Camp Sanitation

Next to eating clean, well-prepared foods, good camp sanitation is most important in preventing digestive ailments. Be sure your cook is clean and healthy. If the cook has a cold or an open running sore on the hands or face, it might be a good idea to give him or her a couple of days' rest. Bacteria can be transferred from the cook to the food and eventually to other campers, causing digestive ailments.

Also, all cooking utensils should be sterilized with boiling water and a detergent. An easy way to do this is to punch some holes in the bottom of a can and rig a bail at the top. Put the washed cutlery in the can and dip it in boiling water.

Boil dishcloths and towels and dry them in the sun. Taking along plenty of paper towels is a big help. Use them to drain fried foods, because solid fats can ruin the taste of food, as well as our digestion. Don't let the cook taste foods and then use the same fork or spoon for cooking without washing it again. The cook may be coming down with a cold or a sore throat without knowing it.

Insect repellent is a must in the outdoors, but insect sprays have caused many problems from the destruction of ozone, to eye and skin irritation. When sprayed directly on foods, they may cause digestive upset and will certainly give the food a bad taste. A good alternative to sprays would be a product such as "Barrier", which is in the form of small paper napkins impregnated with repellent. They are enclosed in a protective envelope about the size of a pack of sugar. They are small and easy to pack. When needed, simply open the envelope and wipe exposed body parts with the damp napkin.

Another problem in the outdoors is the disposal of garbage, which draws flies and tempts animals. Merely throwing it on a fire is not the solution, because it must be at least partially dry if it is to burn. One solution is to dig a deep pit and build a fire in it. Lay green sticks across the pit and place the garbage on them. By the time the sticks burn through, the garbage will be dried enough to burn. Squash cans flat, and crumple up used foil. Bury these and other refuse in the garbage pit.

Before entering any camping or wilderness area, be sure you know the rules regarding garbage and refuse disposal. Some areas will not allow burning or burying; all refuse must be bagged and carried out or placed in containers at various locations.

Food poisoning and other digestive ailments can be easily avoided while camping by using basic common sense. Try to be as clean around the campfire as you are in your own kitchen. Keep opened foods cool or cold, and use them as soon as possible. Never warm up leftovers more than once, and be sure they are untainted. Don't trust water unless you're sure it is pure. If there's any doubt, boil it or treat it with water purification tablets. Remember, taking a few minutes to clean and be careful will help avoid hours and perhaps days of discomfort on a trip.

Hydrocarbons and Petroleum Distillates

All around campsites and vacation homes are substances we never think of as dangerous or poisonous. Yet some of them have the potential for ending our lives or can make our trip or outing miserable. These substances range from gasoline to suntan oil. Most of these are petroleum distillates. When ingested they may cause no symptoms, or they may cause gastrointestinal irritation with spontaneous vomiting and oral chemical burns; pulmonary symptoms, such as coughing or breathing difficulty; and finally depression of the central nervous system, which is rare except for some solvents such as 1,1,1, trichloroethane, or other special hydrocarbons.

Whenever someone has ingested a hydrocarbon or petroleum distillate there is always some disagreement as to treatment. Following are the recommendations of Barry Rumack, M.D., of the Rocky Mountain Poison Center, Denver, Colorado.

For gasoline, kerosene, coal oil, charcoal lighter fluid, lighter fluid, paint thinner, and turpentine if an ounce or more has been ingested, vomiting should be induced.

For mineral seed oil and furniture polish DO NOT INDUCE vomiting because there is no evidence that they are absorbed from the gastrointestinal tract, yet they have the highest risk of causing severe aspiration pneumonitis. The greatest or primary toxic potential of petroleum distillates is aspiration into the lung, with effects on the nervous system a close second.

The following agents are considered nontoxic: asphalt, tar, motor oil, transmission oil, household oil, grease, mineral oil, laxatives, baby oil, suntan oil, fuel oil, and diesel oil.

If it is necessary to induce vomiting, syrup of ipecac is the best choice. Purchase some at your drugstore and follow the directions. Avoid emetics such as salt water. Remember that pesticides are often dissolved in petroleum distillates.

While we are talking about petroleum distillates, Tom adds, "I'd like to give a warning about the dangers of gasoline." Never start a fire with gasoline, kerosene, or similar flammable liquid. Use starter fluid, and allow it to soak in before lighting. Never add starter fluid after the fire has been ignited. Remember, that can of starter fluid in your hand is a potential fire bomb.

Never transport gasoline in the trunk of a car. Even in a safety can, it may still explode. A one-gallon can of gasoline has the explosive potential of five sticks of dynamite!

Insecticides are a common item around most campsites. Most commercial products, even when sprayed directly on food, will probably only cause bad taste and an irritated stomach. Industrial pesticides are a much more serious problem and, if exposed to these, a person should seek medical advice or call the National Pesticide Telecommunication Network at the toll-free number: 800-845-7633. A little time spent on a safety may save a lot of time and money in the local emergency room.

14

Poisoning from Dangerous Plants

Take notice all ye goode men of England. Here lies a mushroom hunter.

From an English tombstone inscription

Outdoorspeople are rarely mortal victims of poisonous plants, simply because they seldom eat what is unfamiliar. However, contact dermatitis from poison ivy, poison sumac, or poison oak is more common but seldom repeated, one episode being sufficient. This section, then, is really for the novice who thinks he or she knows the plant kingdom and is willing to risk anything to prove it. Since we can't stop such a person, maybe a few pictures and words of advice can slow him or her down.

The good word on dangerous plants comes from Zep Stein, R.Ph., research pharmacist for the Poison Control Center at Rush-Presbyterian-St. Luke's Medical Center. Zep's outdoor activities have taken him from the Orient to the Middle East. His work has made him an authority on poisons of all kinds.

Mushrooms

Most plant fatalities are mushroom related. Every year scores of people become seriously ill, and some die, from the effects of poisonous mushrooms. Error is often the reason for picking either an unfamiliar mushroom or one that looks like a nontoxic species. Depending upon the mushroom and the dose (amount eaten), the results can be catastrophic.

Amanita muscaria (Fly Agaric)

Victims are usually children who cannot tell one

Three varieties of poison Mushrooms

mushroom from another. Although fatalities are few, the toxicity is real enough. Usually the victim will experience severe nausea and gastrointestinal upset. By the time the symptoms occur, the mushroom has passed beyond the stomach, where vomiting can no longer be induced by irritants. However, vomiting is sometimes beneficial to remove any residual mushroom still in the stomach and can be induced by gagging or with syrup of ipecac. If syrup of ipecac is used, follow the directions carefully. Anyone who eats or even thinks he or she has eaten a poisonous mushroom must be seen immediately by a physician. The symptoms of mushroom poisoning often resemble those of food poisoning and can even mimic other diseases. Before we leave *Amanita muscaria,* we should be aware that it can sometimes cause hallucinations and/or faintness.

Amanita Verna (The Destroying Angel)

Amanita verna is probably the deadliest mushroom in the United States, although some near relatives such as *Amanita phalloides,* a green-capped mushroom now found in America, and *Amanita virosa* are equally as toxic. In fact, *Amanita verna* is so poisonous that one cap can be fatal. Often the victim of a poisonous mushroom does not know he or she is ill for hours or even a day or more after ingestion. By then, it may be too late. *Amanita verna* accounts for at least half of all American mushroom fatalities.

Other Amanitas

Although there are edible members of the genus *Amanita,* the whole genus is best avoided because of the difficulty in distinguishing one species from another. If mushroom poisoning is diagnosed or even suspected, the Rocky Mountain Poison Control Center can often give advice. Call (303) 893-7771.

Coprinus atramentarius (Common Inky Cap)

Coprinus atramentarius is edible, but *not with alcohol.* The combination can make you sick.

Russula emetica (Toxic Russula, vomit mushroom sickening Russula)

Russula emetica tends to resemble edible relatives. Its red color can fade in wet weather, making it difficult to identify. Ingestion usually causes nausea, vomiting, and diarrhea.

Gomphidus vinicolor (Bad red)

Ingestion of *Gomphidus vinicolor* can cause severe gastrointestinal upset.

Concluding Comments on mushroom poisoning

Most mushroom poisonings occur either in the summer or early fall. The best advice that we can give is to avoid any mushroom that you are the least bit uncertain about. Children must be warned at an early age never to pick and eat these plants. Our listing above by no means exhausts all of the known toxic mushrooms. Other toxic mushrooms of interest are *Gyromitra (Heliella) gigas,* which is edible for some but probably not worth the risk, and *Clitocybe illudens,* which may resemble the edible chanterelles. An exhaustive study of mushrooms can be made by reading A.H. Smith's book *The Mushroom Hunter's Field Guide* (University of Michigan Press, 1963).

Plants Causing Contact Dermatitis (rash)

Many outdoor plants can cause a contact dermatitis, even ornamental ones like English ivy *(Hedera helix)*. Most common are poison ivy *(Rhus radicans)*, poison oak *(R. toxicodendron)*, and poison sumac *(R. vernix)*.

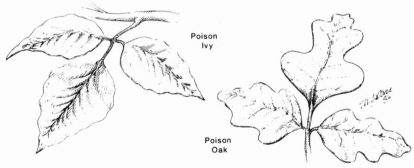

Illustration of Poison Ivy and Poison Oak leaves

TREATMENT

Wet dressings of *Burow's solution* (aluminum acetate) diluted 1:10 for adults or 1:20 for children will relieve symptoms, but treatment of any kind *does not* radically shorten the length of the affliction. Burow's solution is best prepared by a pharmacist, and we recommend this. However, see a physician first if possible. Washing the area immediately after contact with a washcloth will not remove the toxin but may prevent its spread to adjacent areas. Avoid contact with eyes. Ingestion of poison ivy, poison oak, or poison sumac is serious and must be attended to by a physician. It is worth mentioning that these plants can "get you" even when they are dried up and dead, since the toxins remain. If you burn them, *avoid the smoke.*

Plants Toxic when Ingested

Datura stramonium (Jimsonweed)

Jimsonweed is a common poisoner of children, who are often attracted to its berries. Symptoms can be mild or serious, depending on the amount ingested. Serious symptoms include high fever, dilated pupils, and even hallucinations. The victim may be unsteady, confused, and exhibit a rash. A weak but rapid pulse often occurs.

TREATMENT

If ingestion is recent, induce vomiting. A physician's care is necessary. Keep victim quiet with reassurance. For high fever sponge with lukewarm water.

Hemlock (Water Hemlock—*Cicuta maculata*)
          (Poison Hemlock—*Conium maculatum*)
          (Picture)

Both hemlock plants are dangerous. The root of the water hemlock has been mistaken for North American ginseng. Both plants can cause severe gastrointestinal upset and even convulsions. Induce vomiting (if it has not already occurred) and get the victim to a hospital.

Phytollaca Americana (Poleweed, American Pokeweed, Inkberry)

All portions of this plant should be considered toxic, although the mature leaf is considered edible if properly cooked and mature berries have been used in making pies. Raw berries, however, are dangerous. The leaves must be parboiled, with disposal of both the first and last cooking waters, to detoxify the leaves, but problems can still occur even when everything is assumed right.

Symptoms, which include vomiting, cramping, diarrhea, eye problems, sweating, and vertigo, may be delayed up to 2 to 5 hours. In its initial stages, the victim may just feel "unwell". For the victim, vomiting should be induced if it has not occurred and a physician should be consulted at once. The nearest hospital emergency room is your best bet.

CONCLUDING COMMENTS

Certainly, an exhaustive study of toxic field plants is outside the scope of this chapter. Prevention is 99% of the cure in any toxic ingestion. It is advisable to carry syrup of ipecac in your first-aid kit to induce vomiting. Follow the directions carefully, and keep all medications out of the reach of children. Remember, the nearest hospital emergency room is the best place to treat a poison victim thoroughly. The outdoorsperson can often do little except induce vomiting and seek a physician. Vomiting should not be induced in an unconscious victim or when strong acids or alkali have been ingested. However, the induction of vomiting will always carry some risk of aspiration.

Below are some other field plants with reported toxicity upon the ingestion of certain parts of the plant. For additional information, a poison control center should be consulted. The common names are as follows:

1. Buckeye (seeds, leaves, flowers, immature sprouts)

2. Mandrake (also called May apple) — fruit

3. Elderberry (leaves, stems, root, uncooked berries)

4. Buttercup (all parts)

5. Milkweeds (leaves and sap)

6. Death camus (bulb)

7. Oleander (all parts)

8. Lobelia (avoid all parts)

9. Kentucky coffee tree (avoid all parts)

10. Jack-in-the-pulpit, fake turnip (avoid all parts, especially the root)

11. Chinaberry (avoid all parts, especially the berries)

12. Coyotillo (leaves and berries) — Plant also called "Tullidora"

13. Wild balsam apple, balsam pear, poison or bitter gourd (avoid all parts)

14. Yew (avoid all parts)

15. Rhubarb (leaves are toxic)

16. Apples (don't chew large amounts of seeds)

17. Cherries (only the fruit is edible, not the seeds, leaves, etc.). The same is true for plums, peaches, and apricots.

18. Laurels (all kinds—avoid all parts)

19. Mistletoe (avoid all parts)

20. Nightshades (avoid all parts)

21. Potatoes (avoid eating potatoes with many sprouts. Potatoes are members of the nightshade "family."

22. Senna-bean (avoid all *Sesbania* species)

23. Moonseed or moonflower (fruit sometimes confused with grapes. Seed is toxic, but avoid the entire plant).

24. Larkspur (avoid all parts)

25. Locust trees (avoid all parts)

Although this article has mentioned the most deadly and the most common dangerous plants you may encounter, there are many others we have not mentioned. So the best advice is: don't sample any plant with which you are not completely familiar. Let's go over the two items recommended for your emergency kit:

1. Syrup of ipecac   2. Burow's solution

They can be obtained from your pharmacy. "If you ever have a poison emergency," Zep concludes, "you can also get advice by calling the Rush-Presbyterian-St. Luke's Poison Control Center at 312-942-5969. This is a number you should keep available in your home.

15

Poisoning From Spiders, Snakes and Coelenterates

Before we start this chapter, let us all understand that the lay person is not equipped or trained to treat venomous bites (spiders, snakes) or venomous stings (coelenterates or jellyfish). The victim must always be brought to a medical facility. The wise sportsperson will have a citizen's band radio with which he or she can contact help when necessary. Don't forget—seek medical attention and never mind what you saw in the movies.

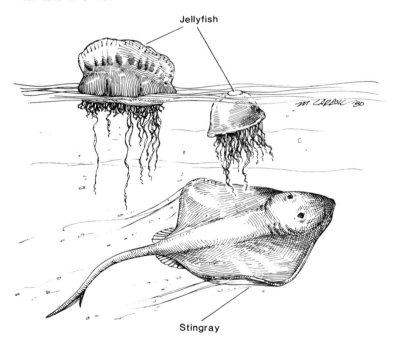

Jellyfish

Stingray

Spiders

The Black widow *(Latrodectus mactans)*

Here is a perfect example of the female of the species being more deadly than the male. The black widow spider at maturity is approximately 1½ to 2 inches long with legs extended. She has a red or red-orange hourglass figure on the under side.

The black widow is usually found under logs and large rocks or in outdoor toilets. She is also a common inhabitant of barns, garages, and basement storage areas. Many bites occur when campers utilize "outhouses" and are bitten on embarrassing areas of their bodies.

Once the bite occurs, there is usually immediate pain, which can last for hours. Many of the symptoms depend, of course, on the area bitten. Muscle spasm is common, and abdominal muscles assume a boardlike rigidity. The victim may have difficulty in breathing and will almost always be nauseated. Treatment consists of antivenin, intravenous 10% calcium gluconate, and possibly, muscle relaxants. Treating a venomous spider bite is a physician's work. The victim's friends can help by washing the bite with some germicidal solution and by arranging quick transport to the nearest medical facility. Do not let the patient smoke or drink. Also, applying suction to the wound and the use of tourniquets is of controversial value. If a tourniquet is used, however, do not *make it too tight*, and totally release the pressure for 2 minutes of every 10 minutes. A misused tourniquet, especially in a person who has poor circulation to begin with, is extremely dangerous. Once again, the actual value of tourniquets is controversial, but if you do use one, a rubber band is the best for poisonous bites, and do not make it too tight.

Brown Recluse Spider *(Loxosceles reclusa)*

The recluse spider is dangerous because it tends to hide in shoes and clothes. Although not aggressive, it will bite when trapped in a shoe or a sleeve. The recluse is also found outdoors. This spider is so common that it is surprising that its bites do not occur more frequently. The recluse spider, also called the fiddleback spider, is about the size of a quarter, but some can be as large as a half-dollar. It has a violin-shaped (or fiddle-shaped) marking on its back. Unfortunately, there is no satisfactory treatment for the bite of the recluse spider. Hydrocortisone succinate (Solu-Cortef) may be given intravenously, but the value of this is uncertain. No antivenin is available as of yet. Skin grafts are often necessary and the wound may take months to heal, thus making the recluse spider a creature to be avoided. Unlike that of the black widow, the bite of this spider is usually initially *painless.*

OTHER SPIDERS

A large number of spiders may produce an irritating bite with discomfort lasting from a few hours to days. The physician may give the spider-bite victim a tetanus shot, providing the victim has no known allergies to the toxoid. Persons bitten by a certain spider can develop a serious allergy to additional bites. Most non-widow or non-recluse bites require no treatment.

Scorpion *(Centruroides sculpturatus)*

This scorpion is found in and around Arizona. Its bite can make one quite ill. Like all scorpions, it has a stinger at the tip of the tail. If bitten, consult a physician. Apply ice to the wound, if possible and take an oral antihistamine (Chlortrimeton 4 mg). With a scorpion bite, antihistamines are not absolutely crucial, and men with severe prostate enlargement should avoid them. Antihistamines will reduce your ability to sweat (dangerous in hot climates), and will also make you drowsy, so let a companion drive if possible.

Insect Stings

If you have no allergy to the stings, they are of only brief discomfort. However, a single bee sting can kill a sensitive individual. If you are allergic to the bite of a certain insect, see your physician about getting desensitized before going on your vacation. Follow the physician's recommendations to the letter. He or she may fix you up a personal allergy kit.

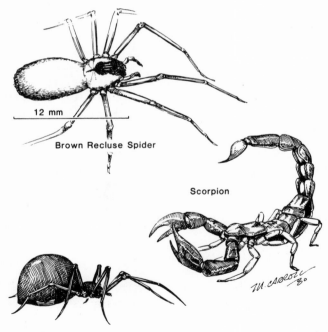

12 mm

Brown Recluse Spider

Scorpion

Black Widow Spider

Snakebites

The American Outdoorsperson may have to contend with rattlesnakes, copperheads, coral snakes, moccasins, and perhaps, Pacific sea snakes.

Campers must familiarize themselves with poisonous snakes in the camping area. The park ranger and local sporting goods stores are good sources. Look at the pictures of local harmful snakes. When camping or hiking, shake out your boots in the morning or at

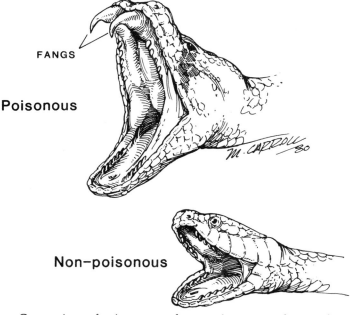

FANGS

Poisonous

Non-poisonous

Comparison of poisonous and non-poisonous snake mouths

any time you have taken them off, but don't shake them over your lap. Avoid reaching into dark areas, and watch where you step.

If bitten by even a nontoxic snake, consult a physician, since the bite can get infected. Suction is of limited value, and a tourniquet, if used at all, must not be too tight. Release the pressure for 2 minutes of every 10 minutes if you decide that a tourniquet is necessary. Get the victim to the nearest medical facility.

Jellyfish *(Portuguese Man-of-War)*

When swimming, avoid these creatures. Don't even touch dead ones on the beach. Remove the victim of a sting from the water, and scrape off the tentacles with sand. Use thick gloves if you have them. Splash alcohol over the wound, which "fixes" the jellyfishes' stinging cells so they can't discharge, and then sprinkle on Adolph's meat (unseasoned) tenderizer, which neutralizes the toxin. Since death may result, get the victim to the nearest medical facility. It may be necessary to give respiratory support while on the way to the hospital. A knowledge of artificial respiration is handy in this case.

Stingrays

Stingrays are numerous at the beaches along the Gulf of Mexico. They are hazardous to scuba divers and waders. If one is stepped on, the animal will lash out with its spiny tail and sting the victim. The pain is excruciating. Muscle weakness may progress to paralysis and collapse. Remove the victim from the water and submerge the body part, usually a limb, in hot tap water. The water should be as hot as the victim can stand. The heat deactivates the toxin and reduces pain. Usually, 30 to 60 minutes of heat will do the job. A physician should remove any barb remnants from the wound, and the wound should not be sutured. Narcotics (for pain), tetanus toxoid, and antihistamines may all be necessary in the treatment regimen.

16

Stinging Insect Reactions

Bill and three companions were finishing dinner; it was almost dusk, but the day was still pleasantly warm. Bill went over to bury the garbage from dinner in the same pit they had used for breakfast that morning. He accidentally disturbed an angry wasp who was searching for dinner, and was stung once on the right forearm. The pain subsided after a few minutes, and Bill thought nothing of it until almost half an hour later, when he began to notice itching all over. He broke out in hives, first on his arm, then on his trunk, and finally on his legs. He began to feel as though his tongue was swollen, and he got short of breath. Frightened, his companions rushed him to a nearby clinic, which was almost an hour away. By the time they reached the clinic, the reaction was beginning to subside. Bill had had a lucky warning. Many others are not so fortunate.

Our breathtaking advice on poisonous stings and bites comes from Allan Luskin, M.D., Co-Director of Allergy/Clinical Immunology, Rush-Presbyterian-St. Luke's Medical Center and Professor at Rush Medical College. Allan loves to be outdoors and is an avid fisherman. His information will help you to avoid big problems with little critters. So let's listen to Allan talk about stings, bites, and allergies outdoors.

"Many people are stung every year by wasps, yellow jackets, hornets, and bees," Allan says. Most of these stings result in only a very mild redness and itching that occurs immediately at the site of the sting. This may last from a few minutes to several hours and then gradually disappear. Other victims may have a

153

large local reaction. This is usually greater than 2 inches in diameter and may cross one large joint or two small joints such as the hands or toes. About 1% of all victims have a more generalized reaction, which can be mild, with hives, or much more severe, with nausea, vomiting, pain in the abdomen, wheezing and shortness of breath, tongue and throat swelling, confusion, anxiety, and occasionally shock and death. At least 100 people die every year from insect stings. In fact, more people die from the stings of these insects than are killed by the bites from venomous snakes in this country. Those people who have other allergies, particularly bronchial asthma, seem to be somewhat more likely to develop severe reactions.

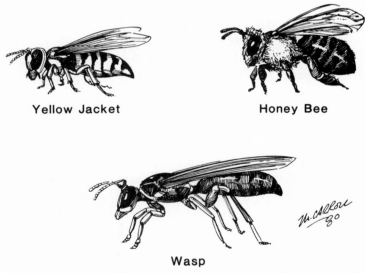

Yellow Jacket   Honey Bee

Wasp

Comparison drawing of 3 stinging insects

Reactions are more likely to be serious in people over the age of 30. Bill's generalized reaction was fairly mild and began about 25 minutes after the sting.

Reactions that occur within 5 or 10 minutes after the sting are generally more severe than those occurring later. At least half of the time individuals have a clue that a more severe reaction might occur. If they have been stung before and have had increasingly more severe reactions, a small local reaction initially, a large local reaction the second time they were stung, and some hives the third time, this is certainly ominous. However, over half of the victims having severe reactions have had no known previous sting, or only a small local reaction.

If a reaction occurs, and the person complains of itching all over, has hives, shortness of breath, swelling of the throat, dizziness, or abdominal symptoms,

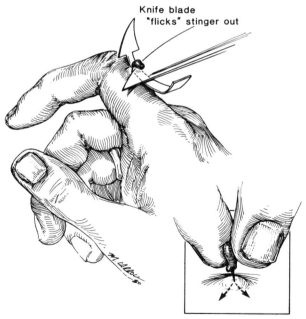

Knife blade
"flicks" stinger out

Trying to remove stinger
manually injects _more_ venom

Technique for removing stinger

immediate treatment is necessary and the closest medical facility should be sought at once.

Of all the stinging insects, only the honeybee leaves its stinger in the wound. If the person has been stung by a honeybee, the vecom sac is usually attached to the stinger and may continue to inject poison for half an hour or so. It should be removed immediately. It should be flicked out with a fingernail, knife, or other sharp object, and should not be grasped between the fingers, since this will squeeze in more venom. An ice cube placed over the sting may retard the absorption of the venom. An antihistamine tablet, which is available over-the-counter (Chlor-Trimeton, 4 mg.) can be taken at the first sign of a reaction, but the major mode of treatment for generalized reactions is adrenalin. While antihistamines may help somewhat, medical attention is still necessary. Patients who have had increasingly larger reactions or previous generalized reactions should seek medical attention, since specific desensitization therapy is available to them. They should carry with them, at all times, a lifesaving insect sting kit. This contains a syringe with adrenalin, as well as antihistamine tablets. If this kit is available, the victim or a companion should inject one dose from the syringe into the victim's thigh and massage vigorously to speed the absorption. A second injection can be used in 15 to 30 minutes if symptoms are not improved.

People who have had previous reactions are best advised to avoid any source of contact with these stinging insects. They are commonly found in fields of flowers and clover. Wasps nest under eaves and are frequently found in and around old cabins. Yellow jackets are ground nesters and are found in rotten tree stumps and in holes in the ground. Wasps and yellow jackets are frequently found around garbage. All of these insects are attracted to flowers and flowered print shirts. Perfumes, perfumed hair sprays, tonics, suntan lotions and cosmetics of all kinds should not be used. Clothing should be light colored, white and tan preferably, since these colors do not attract the insects. Shoes should be worn at all times and insect repellents should be used. An old wives' tale suggests that thiamine, Vitamin B1 (100 mg.), may act as an insect repellent when it is excreted in sweat. The vitamin can be taken once a day for the entire season or used just occasionally when trips are planned.

If one is faced with a stinging insect, move away slowly. Do not swat at the insect. It is best to stay calm and attempt to avoid a sting. A person who is stung, and is not known to be sensitive to insect stings should remove the stinger, which will look like a small thorn or splinter at the sting site. Instructions for removing the stinger have been given earlier. If no reaction occurs, no therapy beyond this is necessary. One can expect all sting sites to become red, swollen, and painful. If the swelling exceeds 2 inches in diameter within the first half hour, however, an antihistamine can be taken. If any more severe symptoms occur (itching at a distant site, flushing welts or hives distant from the site of the sting, sneezing, runny nose, cough, shortness of breath, or swelling of the throat), then antihistamines should be taken and the victim should be brought to medical attention immediately.

If a person known to be sensitive is stung on an arm or a leg, a tourniquet can be placed between the area of the sting and the heart. It should be tied gently. Again a rubberband makes the best and safest tourniquet. It should be loosened for a few minutes every 15 minutes so that adequate body circulation can take place. Of course, the tourniquet cannot be used if the sting is on the face or the torso. The stinger and venom sac, if present, should be removed and ice or cold compresses should be applied. The antihistamine tablets (Chlor-Trimeton 4 mg) should be taken immediately. If any of the more severe symptoms mentioned earlier occur, the injectable adrenalin in the insect sting kit should be used. This should ease the symptoms, and the patient should obtain medical attention from the closest medical site.

These recommendations should allow us to live in peace with some of nature's hardest-working and most valuable creatures.

There are other stinging or biting insects that can make life in the outdoors uncomfortable. There are a variety of flies, including the stable fly, the large horsefly, the tiny deerfly, and the blackfly, whose bites are notoriously painful. They can cause marked local discomfort at the site of the bite and can also transmit disease, since these flies move from one animal to another. Therefore, it's important to cleanse the area around the fly bite thoroughly to reduce the possibility of infection. Several allergic reactions to flies are rare while local reactions are common. In general, a mild antibiotic ointment such as Bacitracin can be effective. A steroid ointment, which can be obtained from physicians and has multiple uses in the outdoors, can also be used. If the itching and redness are marked or if hives do occur around the site of the bite, antihistamine tablets such as Chlor-Trimeton, recommended previously, can be helpful in reducing the symptoms.

These recommendations are also helpful for the bite of the mosquito. Vigorous use of insect repellent is of great help in decreasing the number of bites of these hungry little creatures.

The chigger is a mite that infects people walking

through grass or underbrush. The tiny red, hairy larva crawls onto the skin, usually on the legs, pierces the skin, and secretes an irritating saliva that allows it to burrow under the skin. A tiny pinprick bite may increase to a red area the size of a nickel and itch for days. The chigger falls off after several days, but the red, irritated area can persist. A combination antibiotic and steroid ointment is frequently helpful in relieving the symptoms.

Tick

Ticks are found in all parts of the United States. Where chiggers usually fall off after several days, the tick may cling to the victim for weeks. It is firmly attached to the skin, and attempts at picking it off will usually remove the body and leave the mouth imbedded in the skin. This also will inject more toxin into the area. Therefore, it is recommended that the tick be removed by touching the hot tip of a cigarette to its body or by putting a small drop of gasoline or kerosene on its head. After 10 minutes, the head will usually have disengaged, and removal is generally easy.

There are thousands of different spiders in the United States, but the bites of only two of them are of danger to us. These two are the black widow and the brown recluse spider. The brown recluse is primarily an indoor spider, although it is occasionally found in piles of leaves and under rocks, and its bite is much less frequently fatal than is that of the black widow. The brown recluse bite, however, causes a great deal of local tissue damage, and it may take several days for the damage to become fully apparent. Usually there is only a mild stinging sensation at the time of the bite, which is followed by a slightly larger area of redness in a couple of hours. After several more hours, a fluid-filled bleb may form, and there may be circles of redness creating a bull's-eye-like pattern. At this point it is usually clear that something more severe than a tiny bite has happened and medical care is necessary. However, by this time significant local damage has already occurred. Therefore, if the spider can be recognized at the time of the bite by the coloring and the brownish violin-shaped markings on its back, early medical attention may decrease the amount of swelling and tissue damage.

The black widow is a more dangerous spider who lives in woodpiles and sheds and has been a notorious frequenter of outhouses. Both the male and female can bite, but the female is much larger and has much greater amounts of venom. She is also much more easily recognized by her black body with the red hourglass mark on the abdomen.

The black widow bite is more painful than that of the brown recluse, and a sharp pinprick and stabbing pain is noticed. This is usually followed by a numbing sensation that spreads upward across the abdomen or across the chest over the next hour. The toxin in the bite causes severe muscle cramping along with headache, restlessness, dizziness, perspiration, and weakness. If a black widow bite is suspected, ice should be put on the site of the bite, and the victim should be kept warm. Medical attention must be sought immediately, since an antivenin is available.

There is much confusion concerning first aid for the victims of snake bites because of the difficulty in determining whether venom has been injected through the site of the bite and whether the snake was truly venomous. All snake bites should be treated as emergencies. If possible, and without danger, the snake should be killed and brought with the victim to the nearest medical facility. First-aid should consist of splinting the affected extremity, placement of a rubber band or loose tourniquet between the bite and the heart. Incision and suction is only effective if applied within 10 to 15 minutes after the bite occurs. Two small incisions are made at right angles to each other directly through the fang marks with the razor blade.

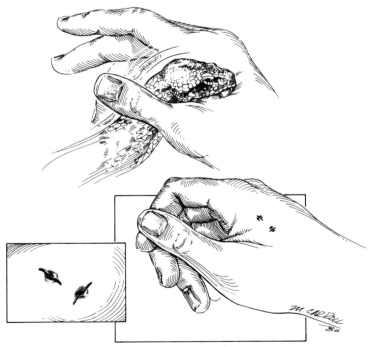

Incisions over fang marks are at right angles to each other

They should be a quarter of an inch long and an eighth of an inch deep. Kits are available with cups to apply suction over the marks made by the razor blade. Mouth suction will do if a suction cup is not available. However, incision and suction are of little benefit 15 minutes or more after the bite has occurred and are certainly no substitute for speedy medical attention.

17

Rashes and Allergies

The misery of hay-fever symptoms—runny nose, itchy eyes, sneezing, and nasal congestion—affects 40 million of us in this country. Staying inside away from pollen and mold spores is the most effective way of treating this troublesome problem. This is totally impractical, however, and takes away much of the enjoyment of nature. There are certainly some things that can be done to make the outdoors more pleasurable for hay-fever sufferers. Where else can we go for advice but back to the professor on allergy, Dr. Allan Luskin?

"There is a wide variety in the seasonal and geographical distribution of outdoor substances causing allergic problems," Allan tells us. For instance, in Middle America the tree pollen season is in the spring, the grass pollinates in the summer and August, and September symptoms are due to ragweed pollen Mold spores are present from the spring through the late fall, but mostly from July through October. There is little, if any, ragweed in the Pacific Northwest and Southwest, but the grass pollen season may be almost year round. In New England, birch tree pollen is a major antigen that is not found in much of the rest of the country. Therefore, if you know what a companion is allergic to, plan outdoor vacations at times other than his or her dangerous pollen season. This is the first and perhaps the most important step in helping an outdoorsperson who is one of the many allergy sufferers in this country.

The symptoms of allergies which affect both the eyes and the nose are relieved by two major categories of medication; antihistamines and decongestants. These are available — over-the-counter, either alone or in combinations. More potent medications in both these categories are available by prescription. Antihistamines such as Chlor-Trimeton or decongestants such as Pseudo-Bid can be tried alone. Antihistamines are useful for relief from the sneezing and runny nose associated with allergies. Decongestants such as Pseudo-Bid are helpful when nasal congestion is the predominant symptom. Occasionally, combinations of these medications, which are marketed as over-the-counter medicines for allergies, colds, and sinusitis, are more effective than either of the components alone. The major side effect of antihistamines is drowsiness, and decongestants will occasionally cause nervousness. These side effects usually disappear when medication is taken on a regular basis over a day or two. Furthermore, these medications seem to increase their effectiveness when taken on a regular basis such as three or four times a day over several days. Therefore, the allergy sufferer is definitely advised to take medication when outside on a regular basis without waiting for the symptoms to start.

Topical sprays are available over-the-counter for relief of nasal congestion. All of these topical sprays shrink the mucous membranes of the nose, but when the effect of the medication wears off, the mucous membranes swell again, frequently to a greater extent than before. This is called a rebound effect, which can lead to repeated use of the medication and addiction. These drugs should be used for no more than two or three days, or a vicious cycle is set up, which results in nasal symptoms due to the medication itself. Long-term use of these medications can cause serious and permanent damage to the nasal mucous membranes. If antihistamines and decongestants taken orally do not control the symptoms, physicians can prescribe other nasal sprays based in cortisones, which are safe, reliable, and nonaddicting. Should these also fail to control symptoms, a course of desensitization therapy can frequently make next year's season much more tolerable.

Occasionally, the allergy symptoms may extend into the lower respiratory tract, causing wheezing, shortness of breath, cough, and sputum production. When this occurs on a repeated basis, the diagnosis of allergic asthma is usually made. This can be treated by the use of drugs that dilate the bronchial tubes. These drugs are much more effective than cough suppressants or expectorants and may either be inhaled or taken by mouth. Patients with a known tendency towards lower respiratory symptoms should contact their physician prior to leaving on trips involving exposure to substances they might be allergic to. Frequently, an inhaled spray or an occasional oral medication is quite sufficient to make one comfortable, even in times of high pollen exposure. If physician advice is not available, an over-the-counter inhaled spray or oral medication can occasionally suffice until more definitive therapy is available. The sprays should not be used more than three or four times per day because these drugs can lose their effectiveness with overuse and can cause a rebound worsening of the respiratory symptoms. They are valuable however, for intermittent use and are frequently successful in controlling the cough and wheeze of allergic asthma.

Ragweed, grass, and trees are not the only plants to cause problems for the outdoorsperson. A whole variety of plants can cause severe and incapacitating skin problems. The three primary offenders are poison ivy, poison oak, and poison sumac. These plants are closely related to one another, and all cause the same kind of skin lesions. These may be limited to a small area of the skin or may be generalized over the entire body. Even when the rash is limited, it can be quite bothersome, particularly when it affects the face or the genitalia.

The typical rash is highly irritating with severe itching, burning, and swelling. These symptoms frequently do not begin until 24 to 48 hours after exposure and may not reach their peak for several days after that. Actual contact with the plant is not always necessary. A dog traveling through brush containing poison ivy or poison oak can carry enough of the oil from the leaves to cause symptoms in the owner and handlers. Once the rash begins, it is not contagious and usually doesn't spread to other parts of the body. Some of the oil may still remain on the skin, and therefore, when the first redness and itching appears, the affected areas and clothing should be washed thoroughly.

Mild symptoms can be treated with cool compresses and calamine lotion. Other over-the-counter topical agents, particularly those containing antihistamines, are no more effective than calamine and can cause skin rashes themselves. Mild symptoms also respond well to steroid creams applied liberally to the affected area several times a day when the lesions first begin, but topical steroids seem to have little effect during the blistering stage of the skin rash. More severe skin rashes due to these plants should be seen by a physician, and oral cortisone is frequently necessary.

Poison ivy, poison oak, and poison sumac are not the only plants to cause skin rashes. Ragweed and a variety of other weeds can cause a rash, which typically occurs on exposed areas, including the hands, face, and a "V-shaped" eruption on the neck. Skin rashes caused by plants other than the poison ivy group frequently occur after exposure to sunlight. For sensitive people, staying out of the sun and using sunscreens seems to be very important. Most important, for the sensitive person, however, is to learn to recognize these plants and to avoid them.

18

The Sportsperson at High Altitude

As outdoor recreation is becoming more popular, an increasing number of enthusiasts are entering environments alien to their usual habitats. One of these environments is the higher altitudes of the earth's surface. Ever since Sir Edmund Hillary conquered Everest, mountaineering has gained in popularity, and with the current interest in skiing, more persons than ever are entering mountainous regions for brief periods of time, including hunters and fishermen. It is necessary to learn a few principles of high altitude physiology to understand the concept of high attitude stresses, acclimatization, and disease.

Our word to the wise on this lofty topic comes from Bruce Greenspahn, M.D., of the Department of Cardiology and Respiratory Medicine at The University of Chicago Hospitals and Clinics. He is a fisherman's fisherman and has outsmarted fish from the Pacific Northwest to Florida's tip. Let's all wet a line together and hear about high altitude problems.

"All bodily systems are to a certain extent affected by changes that occur at high altitude," Bruce says, but the major system affected is the respiratory system. When we breathe, we breathe in oxygen. Our bodies use it to function, and we get rid of its waste products—carbon dioxide and water. The oxygen along with the food we eat is the fuel for our metabolic furnaces. Approximately 21% of the air we breathe is oxygen. At sea level this results in the hemoglobin—the component of blood that carries oxygen—being about 100% saturated with oxygen in a healthy individual. The *oxygen-carrying capacity* of the blood therefore, is a function of the saturation of the hemoglobin *and* the *amount* of hemoglobin present. One can see, for example, in persons with anemia, where the amount of hemoglobin in the blood is reduced, that *oxygen-carrying capacity* of the blood is also reduced. In thinner air, such as may be seen at high altitudes (because the oxygen is 21% of a smaller amount), the problem of significantly reduced oxygen-carrying capacity is more pronounced. Ill effects that might not be noticed at a lower altitude are more readily apparent. Obviously, any person with abnormal lung, heart, or blood conditions may encounter difficulties at high altitude. Since oxygen is necessary for the normal tissues in the body to function, the amount of oxygen being delivered through the blood is important when related to the amount of work that an individual can perform.

As just stated, the saturation of hemoglobin in the blood is related to the amount of oxygen in the surrounding air. As one ascends in altitude, although the fraction of oxygen in the air remains approximately 21%, the barometric pressure is lessened. For example, at 5,000 feet, that amount is about one-third of the oxygen found in the surrounding air at sea level. But, because the amounts of water vapor and carbon dioxide exhaled from your lungs do not fall in direct proportion to barometric pressure, these products make up an increasingly greater percentage of what is within the lung as you rise in altitude and the amount of the other component gases fall. Water vapor pressure remains the same as long as your body temperature is normal, regardless of altitude. Your amount of carbon dioxide is less at high altitude, chiefly because you are breathing at a faster rate. Therefore, the important number is the amount of oxygen in the lung itself. This will determine oxygen pressure and thus oxygen saturation in the blood. One can easily see now, how hemoglobin saturation with oxygen is affected by altitude. The reason that this saturation does not fall in a direct proportion to a rise in altitude is because of the properties of the hemoglobin molecule itself.

The fall in blood oxygen content is the most important factor in determining the spectrum of normal bodily changes, adaptation, and specific diseases that one may encounter with elevations in altitude.

The normal sea-level resident can tolerate an altitude of from 10,000 to 12,000 feet with only a little change in blood oxygen saturation. But, at altitudes greater than 12,000 feet, lowered oxygen content becomes more marked and supplementary oxygen must be used. By breathing pure oxygen, however, a person can attain normal oxygen saturation at altitudes from 30,000 to 35,000 feet, and thus the highest peaks can be conquered. This is because when one breathes pure oxygen, the pressure of other gases is eliminated (chiefly nitrogen) and instead of being 21% of inhaled air, the oxygen fraction is now 100%.

It is important to realize, however, that persons with lung disease will not be able to maintain oxygen saturations at these altitudes. Sea-level residents with these problems would be well advised not to undergo significant altitude changes, especially not without consulting their physician.

The first change that you may encounter upon attaining high altitude is difficulty with night vision. This can occur at even 5,000 feet in elevation and is due to the fact that the specialized cells in the eye are exquisitely sensitive to the slightest lack of oxygen. This is a well-known phenomenon that experienced aviators and mountaineers are aware of, and its existence should be recognized.

At 8,000 feet the number of breaths per minute is increased. This is due to the brain-sensing body receptors that signal that oxygen is low. This reflex of faster breathing compensates to some degree for the reduced oxygen pressure by bringing the oxygen pressure of the air inside the lung to a state more like that of the surrounding air. Because of further bodily adaptations, after a few days at altitude, the respiratory rate increases further. This rate increases in relation to altitude (to 16,000 — 20,000 feet) and with time at a given altitude (up to 2-3 weeks).

The cardiovascular system is also affected by altitude. Acute altitude exposure is accompanied by a rapid heart rate and an increase in cardiac output. But, after 2 to 3 days, the heart rate falls to sea-level values. Altered heart function is still noted, however, in persons new to altitude as well as in those who are acclimatized, when they exercise.

There are also changes noted in the blood. There is an internal mechanism whereby the actual number of red blood cells is increased in relation to the lower saturation of hemoglobin. This results in an increase in the oxygen-carrying capacity of the blood. Therefore, both acclimatized altitude residents and natives can develop extremely high blood counts. This is a slow response, however. It does not become evident for 2 or 3 weeks and can take months to fully develop. This is an important adaptation and can increase work capacity. Under certain circumstances, however, which will be discussed later, an actual decrease in bodily function can develop. A change in the properties of hemoglobin related to certain chemicals in the red blood cell will also develop upon acclimatization and the blood can deliver oxygen to tissues in a more efficient manner.

Because of these and other changes, it has been

found that the actual work capacity is decreased shortly after arrival to high altitude. Only after a 3 to 4 week stay is the maximum work capacity approached, and only after many months, when the red blood cell volume increases, is a greater capacity reached. It is unlikely, however, that the work capacity of a lowlander, even after acclimatization, will equal that of a high-altitude native whose people have been living at that altitude for thousands of years.

There is a finite level of altitude, however, to which we cannot adapt. It has been determined that the highest altitude to which sea-level inhabitants can become acclimatized is 15,000 to 17,000 feet. It was felt by some that the acclimatization attempt during the Everest expedition at 19,000 feet was too high. The men lost weight continuously, even with adequate caloric intake. Andean people generally do not exceed the 15,000 foot altitude in which they live for more than short periods of time, but Himalayan Sherpas have been known to survive for some hours without oxygen even at the highest peaks, over 25,000 feet.

High Altitude Illness

Healthy individuals can tolerate altitude from 7,000 to 8,000 feet without significant symptoms. Between 8,000 and 15,000 feet, all sea-level residents will have symptoms. Acute immediate exposure to high altitude results in the cardiac and pulmonary changes noted, visual changes as noted, and, depending on the individual, headache, confusion, loss of judgement, and possibly fainting. Diminished mental proficiency is first noted at approximately 10,000 feet, and at a 15,000 foot exposure for 1 hour, mental proficiency is tested at 50% of normal. Loss of appetite is also common. These symptoms vary from person to person, and are related to the lack of oxygen. Response is immediate when supplementary oxygen is given. Acute hypoxia must be distinguished from acute mountain sickness and high-altitude pulmonary edema. The latter two are of uncertain etiology and occur after a lag period of up to 4 days.

Acute Mountain Sickness

There is a disorder that occurs in approximately 1 to 8 persons per thousand. It generally occurs with acute exposure at altitudes between 11,000 and 18,000 feet. Cold weather and activity seem to aggravate this illness, and through acclimatization one can usually avoid the problem. It has a tendency to recur upon exposure to altitude and has a time lag usually of 72 to 96 hours. The symptoms can be headache, nausea, loss of appetite, weakness, nightmares, hallucinations, and chest discomfort. The illness generally lasts from 2 to 5 days and is sometimes fatal, with affected persons dying of nervous system complications and coma. Pretreatment with certain diuretics may be effective in some persons, but oxygen, rest, and a return to sea-level are the mainstays of treatment.

High-Altitude Pulmonary Edema ("Water on the Lung")

This disorder occurs at altitudes greater than 9,000 feet in persons not acclimatized to that level and in high-altitude residents who return home after a 2 or 3 week stay at lower levels. There can be a time lag of several days, as in acute mountain sickness. The problem seems to occur most often in young, healthy persons, and is aggravated by cold weather. It usually occurs after rapid ascent to altitude by air travel. When it has occurred once, it is liable to reoccur upon exposure to altitude or, in the case of residents, after future visits at lower altitudes.

The primary symptoms one may experience are related to the lungs: shortness of breath, chest pain, and cough. In addition, one can have fever, a rapid heart rate, cyanosis (blueness of the skin, lips, and nails), confusion, and can be critically ill. Treatment involves oxygen, rest, and return to a lower altitude, with most patients improving. The frequency of this problem is approximately 5 persons per thousand who arrive at a high altitude area by air.

Note that acute mountain sickness and high-altitude pulmonary edema have features in common. It has been suggested that they are variations of the same disorder. They are not to be confused with the symptoms that occur on immediate arrival to altitude, which are due to oxygen lack and are rapidly reversed with oxygen inhalation. The exact causes of these two disorders are still uncertain.

Chronic Mountain Sickness

This is a disorder that develops slowly in subjects continually residing at high altitude. Its symptoms are intolerance to altitude and oxygen lack, in a person who was previously acclimatized. These people develop cyanosis, headache, fatigue, and mental dullness. These abnormalities can disappear when the victim moves to lower altitudes. This disorder is not a problem with sportspeople who undertake brief visits at high altitudes.

Air Travel

Commercial airline cabins are kept pressurized in an atmosphere simulating 5,000 to 6,000 feet of altitude. This does not pose a problem for most travelers, barring a sudden loss of cabin pressure.

Besides the problem of lack of oxygen with a sudden depressurization (emergency oxygen masks are available), there can be a problem with air embolism (air bubbles in the blood) and spontaneous pneumothorax. This is because the air on one's lungs expands quickly as the outside pressure falls. There should be no problem, however, since the air is simply exhaled. If someone is holding their breath at that particular moment, however, or if *noncommunicating* air pockets are present in a *diseased lung*, the expanding air can rupture the lung walls and be forced into other tissues and/or the bloodstream, possibly resulting in death. This is also the common problem with barotrauma while scuba diving and can occur during breathholding during an ascent of little as 9 feet.

The "bends" or decompression illness is a serious condition usually due to prolonged deep sea diving. The cause is the change of dissolved gases in the blood (chiefly nitrogen) from a liquid to a gaseous state that occurs upon too rapid a decompression after a prolonged stay at certain depths. The resulting bubbles in the blood can cause severe pain, tissue damage, and even death. Because of the smaller pressure changes that occur with altitude variations on dry land, decompression sickness is not usually a problem, with the exception of unpressurized aircraft making rapid ascents. Under these circumstances, the problem can be alleviated most of the time by breathing pure oxygen, which results in the dissolved nitrogen rapidly leaving the blood.

When one has been scuba diving immediately prior to flight however, the minor change in pressure *can* result in decompression illness because of the increased level of dissolved nitrogen still present in the blood from the dive. Some authorities, therefore, recommend that divers avoid flying within 24 hours after diving, because exposure to altitude as low as 7,000 feet even after a safe time-depth dive can be a hazard.

All of the conditions of high altitude and related diseases can have more serious consequences in persons with heart and lung disease. Therefore, they should be cautioned when contemplating trips to high altitudes and should consult their physician.

Lung Disease

As previously mentioned, persons with certain chronic lung diseases such as emphysema and chronic bronchitis should be cautioned about high altitudes and should consult with their physicians regarding this and air travel.

Heart Disease

Persons with cyanotic congenital heart disease are cautioned about air travel and altitudes stays and should consult with their physician when contemplating such trips.

Persons with heart disease should limit their activity at altitudes greater than 5,000 feet. Patients with angina pectoris or coronary artery disease should be cautioned about exertion at high levels of altitude, but may travel in commercial aircraft with caution and after consultation with their physician.

Blood Disease

As stated, persons with anemia have a reduced oxygen-carrying capacity in their blood and are cautioned about high altitude exposure.

Persons with sickle cell anemia and sickle cell trait are at a high risk for altitude problems. Cases of infarction of the spleen have been reported in sickle cell trait patients who have flown in unpressurized aircraft, and sudden death in persons with this trait has occurred with exercise at altitudes as low as 4,000 feet.

19

Cardiopulmonary Resuscitation

At 7:30 in the morning on opening day of deer season, a clear, brisk mid-November day, shots were fired from Bob's post. The other four hunters in the camp party, patiently waiting at their posts, heard the shots and were convinced that Bob had gotten his buck, as he usually did on opening day. Around noon, with everyone frozen by now, the party decided to head back to camp for lunch and the truck stopped at the various posts to pick up the hunters.

Sure enough, when the four hunters arrived at Bob's post, there he was, standing proudly beside his eight-point buck, which had been dressed out and dragged about fifty yards. "But, Bob, you should have waited for us to drag that buck out!" was the cry of the other hunters. "Oh, I took it easy, a little at a time," said Bob. Now Bob, being in his late forties, moderately overweight, a heavy smoker, and having a history of high blood pressure, was certain he could still manage to drag out a deer without help.

Upon arriving back at camp, Bob suddenly clutched his chest and complained of a burning sensation, as if his chest was on fire. He also said he felt as though his chest was being squeezed in a vise. Then Bob collapsed in front of the other four hunters, who frantically tried to revive him.

What if this happens in your party this year? Could you recognize the signs and symptoms of a heart attack and immediately react with basic life-support measures? If the answer is no, then I urge you to finish reading this chapter and follow the suggestions at the end. You could save a life!

179

Our story comes from the Upper Peninsula of Michigan, where we'll find Michael Haklin, an avid hunter who teaches cardiopulmonary resuscitation (CPR) and basic life support to the junior and senior medical students at Rush Medical College. Let's join Mike in his favorite place, Camp Snowbear in the Upper Peninsula, on a frosty November night just before the opening of the whitetail season. Pull up a chair near the fireplace and we'll listen to Mike talk about CPR.

When you consider that approximately 650,000 people die each year from heart attacks, and out of that number 350,000 die outside a hospital, usually within two hours after the onset of symptoms, you can then understand the need and urgency for instruction in basic life-support measures to people from all walks of life. This is being done now in many areas of the country, but perhaps the outdoorsperson, regardless of his or her sporting activity preference, should make this a specific point of knowledge and information, since so often he or she is far removed geographically from medical assistance.

Risk Factors

Concerning one's own state of physical fitness, it is important to know the risk factors that contribute to heart attack or heart disease and how they can be altered to reduce the severity of the problem. These risk factors are: (1) High blood pressure. Have your blood pressure checked at least once a year, since high blood pressure is a major factor in heart attack and stroke. If your blood pressure is high, many drugs are available and can be prescribed by your physician. (2) High levels of blood fats. A diet should be balanced and low in cholesterol and saturated fats. (3) Smoking. People who smoke over a pack of cigarettes a day have nearly twice the risk of heart attack and nearly five times the risk of stroke as a nonsmoker. (4) Obesity. Proper diet and sensible exercise will help curb obesity, but a physician's recommendation should be sought for specific diets. (5) Diabetes. Regular checkups and proper medication are required for control. Other risk factors over which you have little or no control are: (1) Stress, (2) heredity, (3) sex, (4) race, (5) age.

Early Warnings

There are symptoms that may indicate that a person is having or is about to have a heart attack. The most common symptom is pain; however, the pain sensation can be confused with indigestion or an uncomfortable pressure or burning sensation in the lower chest or upper abdomen. The victim may feel that the chest is being crushed. The pain may leave and return. It may also be felt in the back or shoulders and may radiate to the arms, most often the left arm, or to the jaw or upper abdomen. If the pain lasts more than fifteen minutes after resting, it may be an indication of a heart attack. Other symptoms that may occur and accompany the pain are: sweating, nausea, vomiting, an awareness of an irregular heartbeat, or fluttering and shortness of breath. The victim will usually feel weak, faint or dizzy, look pale, and have a sense of impending doom, while trying to deny that anything is wrong. Recognition of these symptoms is crucial, since delay of action could result in death.

Conscious vs. Unconscious Victim

If a victim is experiencing the above symptoms and remains conscious, try to make him or her as comfortable as possible in whatever position is preferred. Do not force the victim to lie down, since he or she may prefer to sit. Loosen tight clothing and reassure the victim. At the same time, keep yourself as calm as possible. If the victim has medicine for chest pain, give it.

An unconscious victim will not be able to respond to noise, touch, feeling, or pain. Unconsciousness may result from three things: (1) the victim's airway is obstructed, (2) the victim's breathing has stopped, (3) the victim's heart has stopped. Your emergency response will depend on which of the above conditions you find the victim in.

Critical Time

When talking about an emergency response, you must keep in mind that you are fighting the clock. That is to say that minutes and seconds are critical if the victim is to have any chance at all of surviving a heart attack where breathing and heart action have stopped. Therefore, it is important to know the difference between *clinical* death and *biological* death. By *clinical* death, we mean that the victim is in an unconscious state, does not respond to stimuli of any kind, and breathing and circulation have stopped. What is so critical here is that the brain is deprived of oxygen and generally can only survive for 4 to 6 minutes. It is during these critical minutes that we must begin to breathe and circulate blood for the victim. Beyond this time, brain damage is probably certain, and we call this *biological* death. So it is imperative that you respond within that 4 to 6 minute time span. Refer to the chart.

0 Minutes	4 Minutes	6 Minutes	10 Minutes
Clinical death 0-4 minutes, brain damage not likely	4-6 minutes, brain damage possible	6-10 minutes, brain damage probable	Over 10 minutes, brain damage almost certain

With the above information, let us now talk about

the mechanics of CPR. Cardiopulmonary resuscitation is a combination of artificial respiration and artificial circulation that should be started immediately as an emergency procedure. It is a procedure that, when properly performed, will prevent the victim from entering the biological death zone, thus maintaining basic life support until advanced life-support measures can be initiated or you can get the victim to a hospital. The steps of CPR are designed to be followed as are the ABCs. In other words, when the letters ABC come to mind, they tell you exactly in what sequence you are to respond. Remember, A stands for Airway, B stands for Breathing, and C stands for Circulation. The victim must be approached exactly in this manner, with no deviation. Let us suppose that you come across a victim like Bob, who collapsed in camp. He is lying face down, and everyone around is wondering what should be done. Let us go through the sequences of the procedure used to handle this type of situation.

The first thing to be done is to recognize unconsciousness by shaking the victim and shouting something like "Are you OK?" If possible, send someone for help and position the victim by rolling him or her as a unit, so that they are face up. The total time required to do this should be from 4 to 10 seconds.

With the victim positioned, the ABCs of CPR are now initiated; therefore, A (for airway) is always the first sequence to be carried out. The airway is opened by the head-tilt method or chin-lift method. In most cases the head-tilt method is used (Figure 19-2). Position yourself on the right side of the victim with your right knee across from the victim's shoulder, place your right hand under the victim's neck and the palm of your left hand on the victim's forehead. The neck is then raised and the forehead pressed downward to extend the neck and open the airway. Remove any dentures or partials. If the victim should vomit, turn the head so the fluid can escape. Do not allow it to go back into the lungs.

At the same time that the airway is opened, maintain your position, place your ear over the victim's mouth, and direct your eyes toward the chest and abdomen. We now move on to B (Breathing) of the CPR sequence.

What you are doing here[j] (Figure 19-3) is checking to see if the victim is breathing by looking, listening, and feeling. Since your ear is very sensitive, it is placed over the victim's mouth so that you can more easily hear the breath moving past your ear, feel the warmth of the breath, and use your eye to see the chest and abdomen rise and fall. Opening the airway and checking for breathing should take only 3 to 5 seconds. If breathing is absent, you must begin breathing for the victim by giving four quick breaths in such a manner that the chest does not deflate completely between each breath. This is done by maintaining the open airway position and pinching the nostrils with the thumb and index finger on the left hand, which is on the forehead already and does not leave the forehead. You then make a wide mouth seal over the victim's mouth and deliver four quick breaths, breaking the mouth-to-mouth seal each time because you will not be able to deliver four breaths for the victim with just one of your own. This breathing must be done quickly to maintain an adequate amount of oxygen in the victim's lungs while you determine if he or she has a pulse. (Figure 19-4).

To check the pulse, the left hand remains on the forehead, thus maintaining the open airway position. As soon as the last breath is given, the right hand comes from underneath the neck and the middle fingers are placed on the center of the windpipe (trachea) and slid off into the depression of soft tissue on the side of the windpipe that is towards you (Figure 19-5). The carotid artery is located there and can easily be felt. You can do this on yourself. Always check the carotid artery in the neck and not the radial artery in the wrist. If the heartbeat is weak, the pulse may not be as strong at a distance removed from the heart, but the carotid artery is bigger and nearer to the heart and more easily felt. The time allowed for checking the pulse should be 5 to 10 seconds and should never be hurried. A victim could have a heartbeat every eight seconds, so you must allow time for this important step.

If the victim is found with a pulse but is not breathing, you then breathe for him or her once every 5 seconds or 12 times a minute. If no pulse is found, the C (Circulation) of the CPR sequence is carried out. This is known as ECC, or external cardiac compression. With the absence of the pulse, the lack of blood flow to the brain becomes most critical, so something must be done to assist the heart in its function of delivering vital oxygen to the brain. Remember, we said that for up to 4 minutes without oxygen the brain could still survive, but beyond 4 to 6 minutes, brain damage is probable. So, you must act effectively in producing an adequate blood pressure force to propel the blood to the brain. This is done by moving your knees down from the shoulder to opposite the chest and locating the site for hand placement. The compression is carried out on the lower third of the breastbone (sternum). At the very end of the breastbone is an extension of cartilage known as the xiphoid process. The end or tip of the xiphoid process is felt, and two fingerbreadths above this point puts you on the lower third of the breastbone.

It is important that you draw an imaginary line down the long axis of the breastbone so that your hands will be placed accurately. The point established from two fingerbreadths above the tip of the xiphoid process now determines where you are to place the heel of your hand, and the heel of the other hand is placed on top of the hand in contact with the breastbone (Figure 19-6).

Compression is achieved by rocking forward with the elbows locked and exerting downward forward pressure so that your shoulders are directly over the victim's breastbone (Figure 19-7). The idea is to compress the heart between the breastbone and the spinal column with sufficient force to depress the breastbone 1½ to 2 inches. The compression cycle must be done rhythmically so that half the cycle is compression and the other half is relaxation. To accomplish a smooth rhythm, you should talk to yourself so that you know where you are in the cycle and will not become distracted. There is an easy mnemonic to remember that will help your rhythm. It goes like this: "1 & 2 & 3 & 4 & 5 & 1 & 2 & 3 & 4 & 10 & 1 & 2 & 3 & 4 & 15." When performing CPR as a lone rescuer, you must compress 15 times and then give 2 breaths. In other words, the ratio of compressions to ventilations is 15 to 2, at a rate of 60 compressions per minute. A complete cardiac cycle is a series of 15 compressions and 2 ventilations done 4 times. It will take anywhere from 54 to 66 seconds to complete a cycle.

Now let's talk about the ventilations in between compressions. After the first 15 compressions, you lean over quickly, open the airway, pinch the nostrils, deliver 2 quick, adequate breaths to the victim. Immediately continue with compressions. It should take no more than 5 seconds after the last compression, to give the two ventilations and begin the next series of compressions. After a cycle has been completed, you allow 5 seconds to check the pulse and reassess the victim's condition. If a pulse is absent, you must continue; if a pulse is present but breathing is absent, you must breathe for the victim once every 5 seconds, or 12 times a minute. (Figure 19-8).

The next question is: how long do you continue CPR? The answers are: (1) until the victim is resuscitated, (2) until you are relieved by someone else trained in CPR, (3) or if you are alone with no possibility of help, until you are totally fatigued and cannot go on. Many people may hesitate to compress a victim's chest because they think they might cause an injury or damage to the ribs or chest wall or some other structure. However, even properly performed CPR may result in cracked ribs (the most common complication), but attention to details can minimize many complications. What you must remember at all times is that the alternative to effective CPR is death.

Many thanks to Mike Haklin for his excellent description of CPR. Although our description was of a heart attack victim, the very same procedures apply to a victim of drowning or electric shock. Of course, in the case of electric shock, you must separate the victim from the electrical source before touching their body, or you will receive the same electric current through your own body. Separation should be done with a long piece of wood or another nonconductive material. Only after separation should you touch the victim.

Certainly, you cannot become proficient in CPR just by reading this short article. There are many details to be discussed and shown to you. Therefore, it is strongly recommended that you spend the time to take a basic rescuer's course in CPR through your local Heart Association, Red Cross or fire fighters'

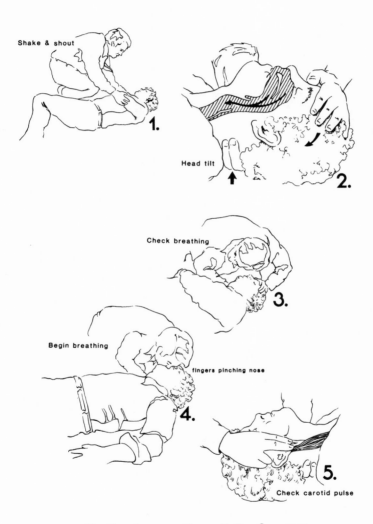

Cardiopulmonary Resuscitation Sequence

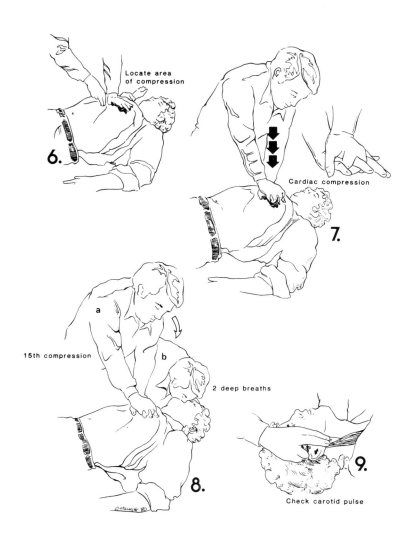

Locate area of compression

6.

Cardiac compression

7.

15th compression

a

b

2 deep breaths

8.

Check carotid pulse

9.

programs in your communities. Using dummy
models, you can learn the mechanics of CPR easily
and build up confidence within yourself so that, if
you are ever confronted with such a situation as Bob's
friends were, you will be able to respond effectively
and efficiently.

20

Problems in the Cold

The most common threat to life and limb that all of those who love the outdoors will encounter is the cold. People who have a lot of exposure to the cold give it a personality of its own. In Alaska, the cold is known as the Hawk. It is interesting that Alaskans choose the hawk to personify the cold. The hawk is a formidable predator who rides the wind to strike quickly and silently—an animal to be respected. The Alaskans survive with the cold because they know and respect its power. Any of us who meet the Hawk in the outdoors must understand and respect its power or we run a very high risk of becoming its prey.

To understand how cold injuries occur, let us look at how our bodies generate and dissipate heat. Our bodies are metabolic furnaces. The food we eat is broken down (burned) in the body and provides energy and heat. The heat isn't just wasted; it maintains the body within a small temperature range in which all the chemical reactions that permit our bodies to function can occur optimally. Our complex chemistry can function well only within a very narrow range of temperature. A particular temperature is maintained within the chest, abdomen, and brain. This is called the *core temperature*. Normally this is approximately 98.6°F or 37°C. The body maintains this core heat as in a reservoir, and the heat is passed on to the blood as it returns to the heart. From the heart, the blood with its core heat is circulated out to the extremities and skin. Temperature control centers in the brain monitor the core temperature via the bloodstream and then regulate it by allowing increased or decreased blood flow to the skin. At the skin, excess heat radiates from the surface, aided by the circulation of air and by the evaporation of perspiration.

There is also another mandatory mechanism of heat loss. When air is drawn into the nose and mouth toward the lungs, rich complexes of blood vessels heat the air and humidify it to 100% to make it comfortably useable in the lungs. Once the oxygen is exchanged for waste gases in the lungs, the air is expelled at core temperature and 100% humidity, and there is a loss of heat and body water. The body, although it is a great piece of equipment, is not perfect, and these forms of heat loss continue even when the body is trying to conserve heat.

Heat generation takes place via metabolism throughout the body, but the real boiler rooms of the body are the muscles. Their high metabolic rate during activity produces a large amount of body heat which, carried in the blood, can replenish the core heat. Now, with this knowledge of what the body can do and also of what it *must* do, let's discuss cold injuries; how they occur and what we can do to prevent them.

Frostbite

The parts of us that are the greatest risk in the cold are those areas most exposed to it. Ears, nose, face, hands, and feet are the first areas to fall victim to cold injuries. Cold air can circulate completely around fingers and toes, and on both sides of ears, nasal structures, and lips, and cheeks. Heat loss occurs very rapidly from these areas, and, in extremely cold weather, heat is lost faster than the circulation of core heat can replace it.

Exposure to damp cold with temperatures around freezing may cause frost nip. Frost nip leaves firm, white, cold areas on face, ears, or extremities. An area of frost nip is usually painful. If it is promptly treated by rapid rewarming, there are no long-term problems. If ignored, the area may blister and peel like a sunburned area and may be permanently more sensitive to the cold.

Frostbite occurs in dry cold at temperatures well below freeezing. An area of frostbite is cold, hard, and white. Although it may have been painful just before freezing, once frostbite has occurred, the area has no feeling at all. Frostbite is the actual freezing of the tissue. Depending upon the extent of the injury, symptoms may subside with few long-term problems. Sometimes the injury can progress to gangrene. Keeping the seriousness of this injury in mind, it is critical that the outdoorsperson possess the knowledge of proper treatment.

Treatment

First, let us put aside the old methods and old wives' tales. Slow rewarming or rubbing with or without snow are absolutely *wrong* things to do. Not only will these so-called treatments not help, but they may actually add to the damage. *No snow,* and *no rubbing!*

For frost nip, the treatment, as in all cold injuries, is rapid rewarming. This can be accomplished by direct, firm pressure with a warm hand or other warm object right in the field. Frost-nipped hands or feet can also be warmed in front of a fire. It is a sign of the most experienced and smartest outdoorsperson to know when to stop to rest and build a fire. Frost-nipped hands can also be rewarmed by placing them in your armpits, and feet can be warmed against a companion's stomach, but by the time you could talk one of your hunting partners into that, it might be faster to build a fire.

Treatment of frostbite is a much more serious business. Frostbite should *not* be treated in the field. An area of frostbite should never be rapidly rewarmed if there is even a slight chance of refreezing. If refreezing occurs, the likelihood of massive tissue death rises dramatically. Also, once an area is rewarmed, it becomes blotchy red, swollen, and very painful. If hands or feet are involved, the victim is not able to use them at all. Since the area is free of pain while frozen, the victim can be comfortably moved to an emergency medical facility as quickly as possible. Once there, rapid rewarming can be accomplished with control of the pain, and the victim can be put at rest.

If it is totally impossible to reach a medical facility, the proper technique for rapid rewarming of a frostbitten area is as follows:

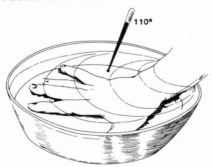

Soaking frostbitten hand in warm water

1. Soak the frostbitten area in a container. If a tub is available, the entire victim should be immersed in warm water with germicidal soap added to it. The water temperature must be between 100 and 110°F because the frostbitten areas are without feeling and are very susceptible to burns. Never

warm a frostbitten area in front of an open fire, there is just too great a danger of a serious burn, which would severely complicate an already difficult situation. Ideally, a thermometer should be used to measure and maintain the water in the right temperature range. If you don't have one, the water should feel comfortably warm but not hot to the touch. The rewarming process should continue until the area or extremity is completely pink, showing a return of circulation.

2. After rewarming, the area will become blotchy, swollen, and painful. The victim should be given aspirin or aspirin-containing pain medications to help relieve the pain; the aspirin will also have a beneficial effect on bloodflow to the frostbitten area. The area should be dried very carefully with any blisters left intact. The area should be treated exactly like a burn. Apply burn ointment (Silvadene or Betadine) and cover completely with a loose sterile dressing to help avoid contamination.

3. The victim must be put at rest with the injured area elevated above the level of the heart to help keep swelling to a minimum. There should be no attempt to move the victim unless this can be done without trauma to the injured part and with absolutely no risk of refreezing.

4. The patient should be kept warm, quiet, and as comfortable as possible and given warm liquids. In fact, warm liquids should be given from the very start of care with rewarming.

5. As soon as it is possible to do so safely, transport the victim to an emergency medical facility.

Severe frostbite is a complicated injury that may require months of medical care. So the best medicine is unquestionably prevention. Try to avoid traveling alone outdoors in extreme cold. Two people should use the buddy system and check each other's faces for signs of frost nip or frostbite. Beards are popular, but they can cover and prevent detection of a cold injury. Stop frequently to rest and warm yourself; build a fire to warm your hands and feet. Don't touch exposed metal with bare skin; this can cause almost instant frostbite in extreme cold. Be very careful handling alcohol or gasoline because they evaporate so quickly on the skin that they will draw off enough surface heat to allow the freezing of the contact area. Don't wear clothing that binds you around your wrists or ankles; this will constrict circulation to your hands and feet. Don't smoke cigarettes in extreme cold; the nicotine causes widespread constriction of blood vessels, especially to hands and feet. Don't skimp when it comes to buying gloves and boots. Buy the best you can, and make sure the boots fit right before you buy them by trying them on over heavy socks. Cover ears, face, and nose in extreme cold. A woolen pullover face mask is a good idea. One last thing: children are far more sensitive to the cold than adults. Their protective systems don't function as effectively and they should be checked frequently and made to rest and warm themselves at regular intervals.

Hypothermia

While frostbite is a localized cold injury, hypothermia is a total body cold injury. We talked earlier about core temperature and the body's heat reserves and heat generators. You know that core heat is stored and then circulated throughout the body. As it is circulated by the blood, that heat is dissipated in a variety of ways. Like little radiators, our bodies give off heat over every square inch of skin. Air currents can carry off the heat. Evaporation of moisture on the skin draws heat out of the body rapidly. Contact with cold surfaces draws heat directly out of the body. We have already discussed heat loss due to inhaling cold air.

When the body's ability to generate and preserve heat cannot keep up with the losses, the body dips into its reserves of core heat. The body will do everything it can to prevent a drop in core heat. As the core temperature starts to fall even one or two degrees, the control centers in the brain dramatically reduce the blood to the skin and extremities, where the heat is being lost. With a decrease of one more degree, the body will begin to shiver uncontrollably with the activity of the muscles being used to attempt to generate heat to restore the core temperature. Uncontrolled shivering should be a red warning flag. If you or a companion has uncontrollable shivering, it is time to get to shelter, or to stop, build a fire, take hot liquids, and get rewarmed.

If the core temperature drops another degree or two, the victim will become lethargic and may be irrational; the quality of the voice may change, and the exhausted muscles will stop shivering. The victim may become stiff. At this point, with the core, rectal, temperature at or below 95°F, the victim is suffering from hypothermia. Hypothermia is and should be treated as a life-threatening emergency. Untreated, the victim will continue to lose core heat. As the core temperature falls, unconsciousness will occur, and at a core temperature below 90°F, severe irregularities of breathing and heartbeat will occur. At or below 85°F breathing and heart action may stop. Start cardiopulmonary resuscitation (CPR) if the victim has gone into or is found in heart arrest. Below 85°F core temperature, however, it is very difficult to reestablish a heart rhythm.

Treatment

When you are outdoors in cold weather, you must know and be looking for signs of hypothermia in yourself and your companions. At the first signs of hypothermia (lethargy, irrational behavior, etc.), emergency rewarming must be started. Give the victim hot liquids if he or she is conscious. Get the victim to shelter. If a tub is available, the victim's trunk should be immersed in 110°F (43°C) water. Arms and legs should be kept out of the water until initial core rewarming has occurred (5 minutes) because the sudden blast of very cold blood returning from the limbs to the heart can cause life-threatening heartbeat irreg-

110°

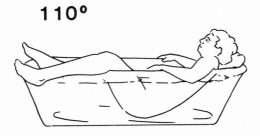

after 5 mins.

Immersed body for Hypothermia

ularities. While the victim is immersed in the 110°F water (head above water, of course) continue to give hot liquids. When the core temperature has returned to normal, the victim should be placed at rest in a warm room and given lots of fluids and a high-calorie diet. Even after complete recovery, the body's temperature control mechanisms will not function properly for some time (perhaps for years) and the victim should limit exposure to cold. This same prolonged sensitivity to cold also occurs in areas of frostbite.

In the field, a warm tub is not always available, so the rewarming process must be carried out quickly with what is available. Get the victim to shelter, build a fire, administer large amounts of hot liquids; these things should all be done as quickly as possible. People who are hypothermic are not generating heat on their own, so don't just wrap them in a blanket or sleeping bag. The victim should be stripped and placed into the sleeping bag or blankets with either clothing and blankets heated over a fire, or another person stripped who can generate some body heat to warm the victim. When placed in a sleeping bag or blankets without some outside source of heat, a hypothermia victim will continue to lose heat, and the consequences could be fatal. If the victim is wet, he or she should be stripped and dried thoroughly.

Prevention

There are things that increase your risks of hypothermia. There are still many people who think that alcohol helps warm you in the cold. That is probably the most dangerous commonly held misconception about the cold. Alcohol is a vasodilator — that is, it opens the blood vessels, especially to the skin, and can dangerously increase heat loss in cold weather. Alcohol does not freeze at 32°F, and, if it is carried in a flask or canteen exposed to the cold, it will stay liquid even when its temperature is 0°F or lower. Taking a slug of 0°F or colder alcohol can cause frostbite of the mouth, throat, or esophagus. This can be extremely painful. The place for alcohol is back at camp with your feet up in front of the fire.

Heat loss by breathing is unavoidable, but wearing a mask or muffler over the mouth and nose can be of some benefit. Heat radiated from the body's surface can be kept near the body by proper clothing, such as inner layers of wool or down to hold heat and a windproof outer shell to prevent or at least limit losses from the wind blowing heat away from the body.

Being wet, whether from rain, a dunk in a lake, or perspiration, is extremely dangerous in the cold. Proper raingear or a windproof, waterproof outer shell in temperatures at or near freezing can make the difference between a good day in the field and hypothermia. Use the layer system of clothing—if the weather warms up at midday, you can shed a layer or two and prevent becoming soaked in your own perspiration. It's good advice to stay dry!

There are other factors that make you susceptible to hypothermia—exhaustion, hunger, dehydration—so rest frequently, eat high-energy foods, and take fluids periodically even if you're not thirsty. Don't eat snow—it robs you of core heat. Special care in the cold is advised for children, elderly persons, people with known thyroid problems, and people with heart problems. All of these have less than totally efficient temperature-control mechanisms and are at increased danger of hypothermia.

The Hawk is just waiting for you to slip up once, so be careful and don't skimp on cold-weather gear. Knowing what the dangers are is the most important step in avoiding them.

21

Problems With the Sun and Heat

All of us who love the outdoors feel a special something stirring within us when we watch the sunrise. It has a unique meaning for each of us—a breakfast cook fire and the smell of coffee, a flock of Canadian geese coming over the blind, the first cast along a weed bed on a still, misty lake. Sunrise—very special indeed— the promise of the day ahead and that good feeling as the sun's first rays warm away the chill of the dawn. We couldn't live without the sun's light and heat, but in its almost unimaginable power there is also danger. If the sun's power is ignored by the outdoorsperson, that power. can burn, blind, and even kill. With a reasonable knowledge and respect of the potential dangers the sun can bring, sunshine on your shoulder will make you happy, just as the song says it will.

Sunburn

So, thinking of sunshine on our shoulders, let's talk first about the most common injury—sunburn. Sunburn is a radiation burn caused by the ultraviolet rays of the sun. Burns caused by the sun can be either first- or second-degree burns. The pigmentation in our skins is a natural barrier to ultraviolet radiation, and the more deeply pigmented an individual's skin is, the more natural resistance to sunburn is present. Protection from the sun's ultraviolet rays is so important that for the sake of survival, nature has made us in many different skin shades, according to our geographic exposure to the sun. The closer you are to the equator, the more direct is the sun's radiant power. An hour of exposure on the 4th of July in Florida will have many times the burning potential of that same hour in July at Hudson's Bay.

The earth's atmosphere is the chief blocker of ultraviolet radiation. At high latitudes the atmosphere becomes much thinner, and there is less to block the ultraviolet radiation. So, any outdoorsperson at high altitude should realize that there is an increased risk of sunburn. Ultraviolet rays are also reflected off snow and water and can add to the risk of burning. Both reflected light and ultraviolet light can injure eyes, so good sunglasses are a must in bright sun and especially on snow or water.

The first- and second-degree burns caused by the sun frequently occur over a large percentage of the body. Persons with severe (second-degree) sunburn will be in great pain, with blistering of the skin and swelling of the burned areas. They will be feverish and feel weak or dizzy. The burned area should be cooled with cool or iced soaks. The victim should be given pain medication such as aspirin or aspirin substitute, which will also help reduce fever; and the areas should be dressed with burn ointment and covered with a sterile dressing. Any large sunburn (10% or greater) on the body surface or any severe sunburn of the face should be seen by a physician.

A severe sunburn is a totally avoidable problem. A wide-brimmed hat and sunglasses can save a summer fishing trip by protecting face, eyes, and neck. A very light pair of cotton gloves can also protect hands from painful burns. Exposure to the sun should occur in short periods at first, so that the body can adapt by deepening its pigmentation, tanning slowly. This will prevent a burn from occurring upon initial exposure. Many severe sunburns occur on a person's first day in the sun. For very fair-skinned individuals in tropical or subtropical areas, that first exposure should be no longer than 15 minutes. Then one can slowly increase exposure time as a tan develops.

There are a variety of sun products that will block the sun's rays and increase safe exposure time. Most manufacturers use a numbering system to indicate the blocking power of the product. The higher the number, the more the product blocks the ultraviolet rays. For example, if 15 minutes unprotected in the sun causes minimum redness in your skin, then the use of a sun screen such as Sundown #6 or Coppertone #6 would permit the same redness to occur after six times as long an exposure, or 90 minutes. Products such as Total Eclipse and Super Shade have ratings of 15 and 17 respectively and would permit longer exposure. Sweating and swimming wash these lotions off, so they must be reapplied periodically to maintain their effectiveness. There are many good sun products, and the amount of blocking power needed should match individual needs, exposure time, location, and season. Very high-exposure areas, like the nose and face, may need special protection with a total blocker like titanium oxide paste.

Heat Exhaustion

All of the body's mechanisms which dissipate heat, and can be deadly in cold weather, are the key to survival in the heat. Heat moves from the hotter area to the cooler area. In the cold, our surroundings are stealing heat. In the heat, however, when temperatures are 90°F or higher, when humidity is high enough to slow down the evaporation of perspiration, and we are exercising, our "metabolic furnaces" are producing large amounts of heat. Thus, overheating can occur.

The mildest form of overheating that can occur is fainting. This usually happens when a person is either not accustomed to the heat or to the kind of exercise being performed. The victim of heat exertion-related fainting (heat syncope) will become dizzy or suddenly tired after exercising in the heat and may suddenly faint. The victim will have cool, sweaty, pale skin and should recover quickly when lying down or sitting with the head lowered. The only treatment necessary is allowing the victim to rest, cool off, and drink extra liquids.

Heat exhaustion is a more serious form of overheating. Heat exhaustion takes longer to develop than heat syncope, often several days, and results from loss of total body water and salt. Prolonged dehydration causes symptoms of thirst, fatigue, elevated body temperature, and finally delirium. Progressive water loss

Heat Exhaustion victim moved to shade

results from sweating and inadequate replacement. As both water and salt become depleted, the victim may develop muscle cramps and other symptoms. As the victim's dehydration becomes severe, he or she will collapse, the skin will be sweaty and cool, and the body temperature may be 102°F. Nausea may develop, and the victim may even vomit.

Treatment for heat exhaustion is to restore lost water and salt and to cool the patient. First, get the victim out of the heat and move him or her to shade or indoors. Give cool liquids; up to 2 to 3 gallons over 24 hours may be necessary to return the victim's water level to normal. Adding a small amount of salt, ¼ to ½ teaspoon per quart, will adequately replace lost salt. If the victim's temperature does not rapidly return to normal, then rapid cooling should be started. The victim should be placed in a bath of cold water or sprayed with water and fanned vigorously to promote evaporation until the temperature begins to come down to around 101°F. The victim should be allowed to rest and should be kept out of the heat, if possible, for a day or two.

Prevention of heat exhaustion is easy. When you are strenuously exercising in hot weather, you must make a conscious effort to drink lots of fluids. For an average person in very hot weather, that may mean 2 to 5 gallons of fluids a day. Most authorities don't recommend the regular use of salt tablets, since most of us take in enough salt in our diets. Salt tablets should definitely *not* be used if there is a limited water supply available.

The most serious form of overheating that can occur is heatstroke. Heatstroke can rapidly cause death or brain damage and is a true medical emergency. Early symptoms are not alarming, but must be carefully watched for during heavy exercise in hot weather. By the way, being in shape is no protection from heatstroke if the exercise is strenuous enough. It even occurs among military recruits doing hot-weather basic training.

Early symptoms of heatstroke include faintness, dizziness, staggering, headache, and nausea—upon exposure to hot weather and exertion. As the full-blown problem develops, a dramatic change in mental status will occur, ranging from confusion and irrational behavior to coma and convulsions. The core temperature will be 102° to 105°F rectally early in heatstroke but may rise in a very short time to 108° to 110°F. The victim's skin will be flushed (red in appearance), hot, and dry, for as the severe late stages of heatstroke develop, the body's temperature control mechanisms are so out of whack that sweating will stop. The heart's pumping mechanism will begin to fail, and the victim will go into shock.

ICE WATER BATH

Heat Stroke victim immersed in cold water

The higher the victim's temperature is allowed to rise and the longer it remains high, the worse the outlook for recovery. Whenever someone collapses in the heat during exertion, heatstroke should be checked for and treated immediately. First lay the victim down and elevate the legs to begin treatment for shock. The victim should ideally be placed in a tub of iced water and the limbs massaged to improve circulation. A tub of iced water is seldom readily available, so use what is at hand, but do it quickly. A cool stream or lake can be used to cool a victim. The victim can be stripped and sprayed with water or wrapped with wet, thin cloth — sheets, for example and fanned vigorously. Try to avoid having the victim shiver, since this will generate more body heat. No matter what, lower the body temperature. Cooling the victim should continue until the rectal temperature is between 101 and 102°F, since further drop in temperature will continue after cooling has stopped. Get the victim to emergency medical care as quickly as possible after the temperature is down. Many problems occurring later can only be treated by a physician.

Heatstroke can be a killer and often is. Even those who recover have damaged temperature control mechanisms and cannot tolerate hot weather for many years afterward. In hot weather, especially with exercise, rest and allow yourself to cool off frequently. Make sure water intake is more than adequate, and give yourself a few days to become accustomed to hot weather if you are a newcomer to it. This alone can eliminate many problems.

Proper knowledge of and respect for the dangers of both hot and cold temperatures outdoors are essential for all of us who use and enjoy the outdoors year-round.

22

Nutrition and Water Balance

The variety of outdoor experiences seems endless, but in every excursion, from the afternoon nature hike to the four-month assault on Annapurna, there is a common factor best expressed by the tandem wails of twin 5-year olds: "I'm thirsty!" and "I'm hungry!" Water and proper nutrition are seldom the primary consideration in most outdoor activities, but they should be considered seriously and carefully by anyone planning to be out of reach of the kitchen sink or the corner grocery for more than a day.

Filling out the grocery list is Robert Passovoy, M.D., past fellow in the Department of Nephrology and Nutrition at Rush-Presbyterian-St. Luke's Medical Center and now Assistant Director of Emergency Services and Acute Care Units. Bob is a backpacking and camping enthusiast, and his writing is chockfull of good things to know about nutrition and fluid intake outdoors.

Many novices in the outdoors, especially those on hunting or fishing excursions planned independently (*not* run by professional trail-guide or wilderness groups), tend to assume that they will be eating heartily each day from the fruits of their efforts. They conveniently (but often perilously) forget that there are days when the fish don't bite, the ducks don't land, and the deer are quicker than the hunter's eyes. Unplanned-for emergencies and even common oversights that would be inconsequential in a state park or preserve, can be at best uncomfortable, and at worst fatal, in a wilderness area.

Water

Water—that is, *potable*, or drinkable, is a primary concern. Under conditions of extreme heat and low humidity, dehydration can be fatal in 2 to 3 days, depending on the temperatures and the amount of activity. The average adult requires an absolute minimum of 500 milliliters (ml.) (about 1 cup) of water as *urine* to excrete poisons and metabolic by-products not removable by other means. This does not take into account the 500 ml. lost through sweat and an additional 300 to 400 ml. lost from the lungs. In general, to maintain normal water balance under *average* conditions (and without exercise), an intake of 1200 to 1500 ml. (1 to 1½ quarts) of water is required. The thirst sensation usually keeps water intake well above this level. The requirement for water increases as activity and temperature increase and humidity decreases. In extreme conditions you may require as much as 4 to 5 liters of water per day to maintain comfort. Activity and heat tend to cause greater water losses through sweat and respiratory water loss (though sweating can be significant) especially under cold conditions and at high altitudes. Cold and dry conditions are the most dangerous, since heat will cause thirst by parching, but major water losses may go completely unnoticed in the cold. High heat-low humidity, such as in the desert, can be deceptive as well, since the water lost through the skin evaporates quickly and is not immediately perceived as sweat. This kind of weather can also make the temperature seem lower than it actually is, and major water losses can be undetected.

Dehydration occurring (when water loss significantly exceeds water intake) causes a number of adverse effects, all of which can contribute to a major problem in the wild. The primary effect of excess water loss is to increase the viscosity of the blood, hampering proper circulation. This slowed circulation hampers oxygen and nutrient flow to the brain, causing disorders of thought, hallucinations, irritability, and disorientation. It decreases clearance of metabolic by-products from muscles, causing fatigue and cramping. It plays havoc with the body's normal protective heating and cooling mechanisms, leading to exposure and frostbite in cold weather, and to heatstroke in hot weather. Dehydration coupled with excess loss of salt can complicate all of the above problems, can cause coma, and, if not corrected, can cause death. Often, this is seen in winter-acclimatized individuals who are suddenly active in high heat conditions and replace their sweat with pure water. Their sweat is found to be *much* saltier than that of heat-acclimatized people. This is something to keep in mind if you live in Minneapolis and take a winter trip to Florida.

Now that you are convinced that venturing away from downtown Chicago (or Pittsburgh, or Beaver's Falls, or wherever) will mean your immediate and irrevocable death by desiccation, how does one avoid this fate? Simple. Drink! How much? The temptation is to steal a line from the old vaudeville comic and say "Enough," because, under most conditions, the sense of thirst, which is the body's major protection against excess water loss, will ensure that adequate water is absorbed. In general, an average 160-pound person, in cool or warm surroundings, with moderate activity, required a minimum of 1,500 to 2,000 ml. (2 to 2½ quarts) of water to maintain a proper water balance. As activity increases or the surroundings get hotter or dryer, the person will need more water, up to 6 gallons a day for desert country or other hot areas.

Winter conditions call for more care, since the

parching effect of summer heat is not present to jog
the memory of thirst. Frequent drinks of water, con-
sciously taken despite the absence of the sensation of
thirst, will help maintain normal fluid balance and
body function. Also, alcoholic beverages do not adequately replace fluid losses because alcohol is a
diuretic and will actually cause the loss of more water
in the urine than was consumed in the beverage. Alcohol, unless used with great prudence, is dangerous
outdoors for many reasons, and it should definitely be
avoided in conditions of extreme heat or cold or when
other fluids have limited availability.

The type of field activity, as well as its location will
tend to determine your water planning, since water is
(a) bulky and (b) heavy. Obviously, a backpacker will
not be able to carry much more than a day's supply of
water under extreme conditions, while a well-
equipped canoeing or boating expedition will often be
able to carry sufficient water for all its members'
needs.

Locations of sources of drinkable water should be
noted in advance and marked on route maps. *Drinkable* should be emphasized, since many natural water
sources are now polluted. Most high mountain
streams and springs remain pure, but water from low-
land sources should be purified before drinking
unless its purity is known.

How do you purify water? There are a number of
commercial water purifiers currently available, most
of the fancier models involving columns of activated
charcoal and ion exchange resins. These tend to be
expensive and clog easily, especially in areas where
the water sources are high in sediment. What's worse,
like most products of advanced consumer technology,
they tend to give out at the worst possible moment.
Sediment can be removed by straining the water

through a fine cloth, and purification is reasonably easily accomplished by boiling 5 minutes at sea level and an additional 1 minute for each 1,000 feet in elevation. If boiling isn't feasible, Halazone or iodine tablets, available at pharmacies, can be used to purify the water. (See Chapter 13).

During the winter, water can be more of a problem, since many open water sources usually available are ice covered or otherwise inaccessible. Snow or melting ice becomes the next best source, carried in a 1-quart bottle, which is refilled each time a drink is taken. Freshly fallen snow or snow that is undisturbed is best. The old and rusty joke about "yellow snow" carries real weight, since many wild animals carry organisms in their urine that can be harmful to humans.

Again, if there is any doubt about the purity of the source of your water, boil it. Probably the most important additions to a winter survival kit are a pot and a Sterno stove.

Food

As mentioned before, expectations often exceed realities in the field, especially on hunting and fishing excursions. The ideals are full-limit catches of fish and fowl and deer that amble obligingly into your gun sights. Meals are hearty and largely composed of your day's harvest, romantically supplemented with natural herbs, roots, and berries from convenient bushes. The reality often involves rotten weather that keeps the fish away, birds that don't even come close, deer that move at twice the speed of sound, and roots and berries that are probably poisonous. A certain amount of planning and care can prevent real discomfort and, in extremes, avert disaster.

In general, shelter and water are the primary considerations in the field. Without them, a human can die of exposure in 2 to 3 days. Without food but with shelter and adequate water supplies, survival can be extended through several weeks since the body is able, to some extent, to live off its own substance.

Food is best expressed as a function of energy exchange. The units used are calories. The body's requirements for fuel and "building blocks" (protein) vary with the demands placed upon it. The basic needs of a 180-pound male are met by an intake of about 70 calories/hour (1,800 to 2,000 calories/day). Those of a 120-pound female are met, by about 60 calories/hour, or 1,300 to 1,500 calories/day. Stress, exertion, and cold will often raise these requirements as high as 600 calories/hour for very heavy muscular work (for example, 5,000 calories for 8 hours of brisk walking with a 30 to 50 pound pack).

Cold weather places unusual stresses on the body, requiring large quantities of energy simply to retain core temperature. Conscientious attention to diet is a must under these circumstances, since low blood sugar levels, fatigue, and incoordination can hit quite suddenly. The staffs of many midwestern ski areas have begun using their public address system to remind skiers to eat, especially on relatively mild days. They find that visits to their emergency medical areas drop significantly as a result.

The fuels available to supply the body's energy demand are divided into four broad categories: carbohydrates (simple and complex), proteins, alcohols, and fats.

Carbohydrates supply 4 calories/gram of energy, the lowest of the four, and are absorbed easily and quickly by the body. In the case of the simple carbohydrates, (pure sugars, candy, pastries, etc.), they are often utilized almost immediately after being eaten. Complex carbohydrates (fruits, starches, vegetables) take longer to digest, but are still easily utilized by the body. For this reason, carbohydrates are considered the best energy source available, and most authorities recommend that 60 to 70% of a person's outdoor diet be composed of a mix of simple and complex carbohydrates. Simple carbohydrates alone are not recommended, since their rapid absorption into the bloodstream in large quantities can cause oversecretion of insulin by the pancreas and an unbelievably rapid drop in blood sugar levels, causing fatigue, dizziness, nausea, and occasionally fainting. Complex carbohydrates supply just as much energy, but their slower absorption time and ease of digestion exert a protective effect on blood sugar levels.

Proteins also supply 4 calories/gram of energy, but are more important to good nutrition for the "body-building" elements they contain. Stress and exertion will create an increased need for protein to repair damage and build new muscle and other body proteins. Sources are meats, milk, cheese, eggs, cereals such as wheat, oats, and rice, soybean products, peas, beans, and other legumes. While proteins are important in the outdoor diet, they are not as efficient a fuel as are carbohydrates, because they require energy expenditures by the body to break them down to energy-producing substances. Proteins also digest more slowly and may impair performance in the field.

Alcohols, though they supply 7 calories/gram, are *not* recommended in the field, since their side effect is sedative, depressant, and they can cause impaired judgement. Alcohols are converted to carbohydrates, but this is not as efficient as using the carbohydrates in the first place.

Fats are the best energy supply in terms of càlories per gram (8), but they are the slowest to digest and the last to be utilized. Actual fat requirements by the body are minimum, with most ingested fat either being broken down for energy or stored as fatty tissue. The value of fats in the field lies in their high caloric content and slow release. Major sources of fats include fatty meats such as pork, butter, margarine, egg yolks, nuts and cheese.

A discussion of menus for various outdoor requirements would require a book to itself. A few basic ideas, however, may serve as guidelines for intelligent nutritional planning.

1. What do I eat?

In general, outdoor activities tend to be strenuous, or at least more strenuous than the normal activity of the participant. The demand of the body is, therefore, for immediate energy through the day and for rebuilding an energy reserve storage during rest periods at night. The day should start with a high energy, light meal—cereal and fruit, or a Granola-type mix. Heavy, greasy, and fatty breakfasts should be avoided, since the stomach and intestine compete for blood flow with the rest of the body while digesting food. The result of a heavy meal combined with heavy activity is often a severe stomachache or muscle cramps.

Heavy lunches should be avoided for the same reason. A better idea is to snack continuously through the day, using high-energy foods. One of the most popular concepts in recent years is Gorp or Trail Mix. Whatever the name, it is a combination of nuts (usually peanuts and cashews), raisins, grains (or granola), coconut, seeds (sunflower, etc.), and chocolate chips in varying proportions. When carried in a waterproof container, it is a portable, delicious, high-fiber, high-energy food. Each region seems to have its own favorite mix, and most health food stores sell their own recipes by the pound, usually at outrageous prices. A number of companies have begun mass-marketing Gorp-type mixes in tiny cellophane bags, but for the serious outdoorsman, the price of these is prohibitive. Your best bet is to experiment and develop a mix that suits your own needs and tastes.

The evening meal is the large meal of the day. It should contain the bulk of the day's protein and fat, and if possible, vegetables and complex carbohydrates. These can include stews, or if you were lucky, the yield of your fishing or hunting. The fats and proteins will digest overnight and leave you ready for the next day's activities.

2. How much food should I take, and what kind?

This depends entirely on the type of excursion you're planning. A large-scale camping excursion involving motorized transport will have a great deal more flexibility than a 1 or 2-person backpacking expedition. In general, don't pack more than you can carry, and *always* pack enough food for several extra days. Good bets for emergencies might well be several packets of freeze-dried meals (a useful offshoot from the space program). Small packets of spices, salt, pepper, and "durable" vegetables (root crops like carrots and onions) are also good bets. Gorp is always good.

3. What shouldn't I take?

Unless you're planning to carry along your own refrigerator, or it's *really* cold out, don't take perishable items such as mayonnaise, prepared foods in "resealable" containers, or "delicate" vegetables.

A final word about fiber. Much has been said and many claims have been made about the benefits of dietary fiber. For the purposes of this book, it should be kept in mind that the average outdoors experience involves a fairly substantial alteration in dietary pattern for its participants. The usual response to sudden changes in diet is alteration in bowel function, usually constipation. The inclusion of high-fiber foods (whole-grain cereals and breads, dried fruits such as raisins and prunes, vegetables, nuts, and, of course, Gorp) in the meal planning will usually tend to minimize these problems.

23

Sharing the Outdoors with Children

Traveling with children can be a unique experience. Even the shy, introverted child and small infant open up to the sounds and sights of outdoor life. Bird calls and the rustle of leaves will draw their attention and bring a new dimension to their understanding of the out-of-doors. Be prepared, however, for the myriad of questions and curiosities that this experience will draw out of them. Your responses to their inquiries will set the pattern for future trips. Your attitude toward conservation, as in everything else in a child's life, forms the basis of the child's future attitude toward protection of the surroundings.

Sharing your enjoyment of the outdoors with your children is a special event for you, the outdoorsperson. Seeing a daughter or son experiencing the special thrill of a first hunting or fishing trip, putting up a tent, or staring into a campfire can bring even greater pleasure to a parent than it does to a child. Kids are not just little adults—their problems require special care. Many topics will be discussed here that are covered elsewhere in this book, but with a pediatric viewpoint. Our pediatric advice comes from Mark Rosenberg, M.D., pediatrician and outdoorsman, who practices in Barrington, Illinois. Mark is as enthusiastic as he is knowledgeable, and he has all the information you'll need to help make a trip with children as safe as it is enjoyable. Let's add one important point: if both parents are going on a trip and children are left at home in someone else's care, the parents should leave a letter of "permission to treat." A letter of "permission to treat" is just a note signed by the parent giving permission for your child to receive emergency medical treatment so that there will be no delay in the child's getting medical care because parental permission is not available. Now let's talk with Mark about kids in the outdoors.

"Any trip must begin with planning and preparation," Mark says, "and this is no different with respect to the needs of children. One should be aware of their past medical history and existing problems. If your child has any chronic medical problems, these should be noted on a record of his or her medical history. A complete physical examination should be considered in the weeks prior to departure, particularly if there has been a recent problem. A statement from your physician should document current problems and provide a list of medications and dosage. One should bring along sufficient quantities of medications to last the duration of the trip. Certain medications such as insulin can merely be kept in a cool location, whereas others may need to be refrigerated. Some antibiotics, if needed, can be obtained in individual dose containers and mixed according to the directions, immediately prior to administration. In the case of diabetes mellitus in children, you can obtain on prescription from your physician a kit of injectable glucagon to administer in the event of a hypoglycemic reaction. This should be carried at all times, particularly if you are some distance from medical care. It is used in the situation of an insulin reaction when the child is not able to take sugar-containing substances by mouth.

One should be aware of any allergies to medications, and these should be documented in the child's medical record or by use of a "Medi-Alert" bracelet or tag. Particular allergies or sensitivity to foods or insect bites should also be known. Management of allergic reactions will be discussed later in this chapter.

Along with preparation, prevention is the key to the avoidance of many problems that may arise during a vacation. Accidents are now the leading cause of death in children, and indeed in persons below 40 years of age. While being aware of potentially harmful agents may be the first step in the prevention of accidents, there are some settings in which accidents are most likely to occur. These include hunger or fatigue, a substitution for the usual caretaker of the child, and changes in environment, such as a vacation. Clearly, an outdoor vacation setting has the potential for accident occurrence.

Prevention of accidents begins before you leave the driveway of your house. Precautions that one should take before leaving include:

1. Lock all doors.

2. Secure all sharp or heavy objects in the car.

3. Do not leave children unattended in the vehicle.

Children over five years of age should use a standard lap safety belt. Children below five years of age or under 20 kilograms (44 pounds) should be restrained by means of a proper child-restraint system. A list of acceptable restraining devices is available in *Consumer Reports,* March 1975. The effectiveness of such devices has been clearly proved, and they should be used before departing on any trip.

Prevention may be broken down into a developmental approach. Infants below six months of age are under direct parental control, and thus accidents generally occur during the usual care processes such as bathing and feeding. Between six months and one year of age, the child is becoming more mobile. While pulling himself or herself to a standing position, the child may pull things down and be injured. Infants below one year of age should be under close supervision at all times.

Between one and three years of age, the child is at the most curious stage. Potentially harmful agents such as medicines, fishhooks, etc. should be kept out of reach. Parents should be particularly alert to the dangers of water and heat.

While the child between ages three and six is able to learn safety precautions, play should be closely supervised and potentially harmful objects should be removed. In particular, caution should be exercised with respect to poisoning, drowning, and burn injuries.

Over the age of six years children tend to explore and with peer pressure may become more adventurous than on their own. In addition to water safety and burn precautions, firearms should be kept out of reach and locked up. Animal bite prevention should be taught, as well as proper respect for wild animals.

In general, common sense and diligent observation can be the guide for prevention of most accidents and without interfering with outdoor fun. The sections below contain guidelines for selected accidents.

Animal Bite Accidents

There is no excitement quite like encountering an animal in the wilderness. For the young child, that may be a squirrel or chipmunk. Infants should be closely supervised in the presence of strange animals, including pets. Such animals may not be accustomed to the curiosities of small children. Older children should be instructed to avoid contact with wild animals or with the pets of others. Examples should be set to avoid feeding strange animals. Frequently, these animals become provoked upon the withdrawal of food and may then attack.

Even though the incidence of rabies has been dramatically reduced in recent years, certain precautions should be taken. Wild animals such as the skunk, fox, raccoon, bat, and squirrel should be considered rabid and rabies prophylaxis given if the animal cannot be examined. No rabies prophylaxis need be given if the child is attacked by a healthy dog or cat. If the immunization status of the animal is not known or if it escapes, however, such treatment should be given.

Rabies is generally transmitted by means of contact with infectious saliva or an open wound, abrasion, or mucous membrane surface. The wound should be thoroughly washed with soap and water. Then it should be irrigated with Zephiran, which has specific activity against rabies virus. Such wounds should not be closed by sutures if contamination with rabies is suspected. As in the situation with any open wound, antitetanus immunization must be considered.

Insect Bites

An outdoor camping trip will invariably entail exposure to the multitude of insects present in the woods. Such insects may produce effects in various ways, ranging from invasion of the skin to injection of foreign material capable of producing an allergic reaction.

Treatment of the common mosquito bite should include cleaning of the area, liberal use of a soothing lotion such as calamine and application of cool compresses. Itching and further scratching of the bitten area may be prevented with oral antihistamines. Sensitive children should be protected by covering exposed areas with loose-fitting clothing and insect repellents.

Allergic reactions caused by stings of bees, wasps, and ants may produce symptoms varying from local

reactions to severe generalized reactions with difficulty in breathing and collapse in sensitized
individuals. Children who are known to have severe
reactions should carry adrenalin kits, and there
should be an adult who is instructed in their use nearby at all times. Currently, desensitization by means of
injections has not been proved to be effective with the
presently available extracts.

Ticks may cause injury not by their bite alone but
by the local skin reaction to portions of the tick that
have been incompletely removed. Symptoms may be
observed due to toxins secreted by the female tick.
These vary from fever, chills, and abdominal pain to
weakness and paralysis. Recovery is prompt—within
24 hours after removal of the offending tick. Ticks
may be removed by various means, including use of a
hot match head or pin or by covering the area with
mineral oil.

Rocky Mountain spotted fever is a bacterial illness
transmitted by ticks and prevalent in the Western
states, North and South Carolina, southern Illinois,
and sporadically in other areas. This severe disease is
characterized by high fever, abdominal pain, aches,
and a pinpoint rash of the palms and soles of the feet.
Treatment should be instituted as soon as it is recognized. If one is traveling in these areas and will be
backpacking, a supply of tetracycline, an antibiotic,
should be carried.

Swimmer's itch is a skin rash often confused with
an insect infestation but actually caused by swimming
in fresh water contaminated by parasites from water
fowl. The rash consists of redness with small blisters
or hives, which is most severe two to three days following exposure. Treatment is similar to that for mosquito bites. Calamine lotion, oral antihistamines, and
in severe cases steroid cream applications.

Burns

The most effective treatment of burns is prevention. Be alert to the presence of small children, particularly when starting a charcoal fire and using flammable agents such as gasoline or kerosene. These agents may pose a double risk because of the possibility of ingestion or inhalation.

Chemical burns should be washed with water thoroughly for at least 30 minutes. No attempts should be made at neutralizing the substance, and the child should be seen by a physician.

Minor burns should be immersed in cool water or covered with cool, wet compresses. The cooling should be continued until the pain stops, and then the burn may be treated by a thin application of an antiseptic ointment such as Betadine ointment. Blisters, if present, should not be broken.

In the case of major burns, one should initially immobilize the child, remove clothing in the area of the burn, then cover with cool, moist cloths. The child should then be transported to a hospital as soon as possible. One should remember that the skin of children is thinner than that of adults and therefore they are more prone to extensive burns.

Head Injury

Injuries to the head are quite common in children. These may result from a blow to the head, a thrown object, or a fall. More important than skull x-rays is simple observation of the child, particularly for the initial 24 hours following the accident. Listed below are some guidelines of when to seek medical attention:

1. Loss of consciousness at the time of the injury or following the accident.

2. If you are not able to arouse the child from sleep. This should be checked at 2 to 3 hour intervals during the night.

3. Persistent and severe headache

4. Persistent vomiting, occurring more than once or twice

5. Drainage of blood or clear fluid from the ear or nose

6. Bizarre or unusual behavior

Exposure Injuries

Children are more susceptible to heat and cold exposure injuries, both because of an inability to protect themselves from the outdoor environment and, from a physiological point of view. Children have a thinner outer skin covering and a proportionately greater surface area for their weight. A few simple guidelines will help you recognize and treat such injuries until medical care can be obtained.

The severity of frostbite depends upon both the temperature and duration of the exposure. This may be influenced by humidity and the wind, both of which shorten the length of time necessary to produce frostbite. In addition, high altitude may significantly accelerate frostbite.

Initially the injured area becomes numb and stiff. With rewarming, the area will become reddened, swollen, warm and, if severely affected, may blister and become gangrenous.

The most important part of treatment is rapid rewarming in warm water (between 104 and 110°F), which should take approximately 20 minutes. Warming in water is more effective than using warm blankets. The affected area should *not* be massaged, as this will cause more damage. Following rewarming, the area should be elevated to minimize swelling. Medical care should be sought if a large area is affected or if blisters or gangrene occur.

Heat exhaustion is caused by loss of salt and/or water, and may occur more rapidly in children, especially during or after exertion. The skin is cool, moist, and pale, although the child has a normal temperature. The child should be moved to a cool location, clothing should be loosened, and liquids should be given by mouth if the child is conscious.

Heat stroke results from a failure of the body's heat regulating mechanism. The child is warm and dry, and the skin is reddened. Body temperature is elevated, often to extreme degrees. The child should be moved to a cool location and the temperature reduced by cool towel applications. Medical care should be sought as soon as possible.

Poisoning

Accidental poisoning is a common problem of young children. The highest incidence is in the two-year-old group, relating to the normal childhood curiosity of this age and increasing mobility. Ingestions tend to occur during times of family disruption, and this includes vacations and the preparations for such trips. Any potentially toxic substances such as medications, cleaning agents, and pesticides should be secured from an infant's reach.

In the event of an accidental ingestion, medical attention should be sought as soon as possible. Until a physician's instructions can be obtained, the following guidelines may be of assistance. The most important information is accurate identification of the substance and the maximum amount that may have been ingested. If possible, labels and samples of the substance should be brought to the hospital.

If there will be a substantial delay in reaching medical assistance, you should initiate treatment on your own. Vomiting may be induced by means of syrup of ipecac, 15 cc. (1 tablespoon by mouth). If this is not available, vomiting may be brought on by mechanical means such as gagging. Vomiting should not be induced if the child is unconscious or if the substance ingested is either a caustic agent or hydrocargon compound. Examples of caustic acids include metal cleaning fluid, toilet bowl cleaners, and some bleach products. Caustic alkalis may include powerful detergents, toilet bowl cleaners, and dishwasher and laundry powders. Examples of hydrocarbons include gasoline, kerosene, lighter fluids, paint thinners, solvents, furniture polishes, and waxes. Medical care should be sought immediately, and if the child vomits spontaneously, attempts should be made to prevent aspiration of the stomach contents into the lungs.

Common Medical Illnesses

The following represents a guideline for the treatment of some common medical illnesses in infants and children. Most acute illnesses can be managed adequately without medical assistance both at home and in the wilderness. Common sense, calmness, and a few precautions should be your guides. Your trip should be delayed or children should be left at home if they have recently been exposed to or ill with such viral infections as chicken pox or measles. Not only will such illnesses make your vacation frustrating and more difficult, but your child may potentially expose other children to these infections. If in doubt as to the incubation period, consult your physician.

Fever

It is important to regard fever as a *symptom* of illness, whose treatment will not resolve the underlying disease process. Children and infants in particular tend to have higher temperatures with illness than do adults, and the severity of the fever does not necessarily correlate with the seriousness of the problem. The normal rectal temperature of an infant is 37.5°C (99.6°F). In general, any child with a temperature greater than 40°C (104°F) should be evaluated by a physician.

The treatment of fever consists of antipyretics (to reduce the temperature) such as aspirin or acetaminophen (Tylenol) and oral fluids. An approximate guide to the dosage of aspirin is 1 children's aspirin for each year of age up to a maximum of 10, or 2 adult aspirins for children of average body weight. This may be repeated at 4 hour intervals. Infants, whose fever does not respond to antipyretics may be sponged with tepid water, but never with alcohol. They should not be given ice baths.

Fever, by accelerating the metabolic rate or energy consumption of the body and the rate of breathing, may cause rapid water loss, particularly in small infants. This, together with warm weather, may produce dehydration if the oral fluid intake is not increased. If there is no accompanying vomiting or diarrhea, this may be accomplished by water alone. If there is excessive salt loss such as occurs with very warm weather, vomiting, or diarrhea, salt should be replaced by means of an oral electrolyte or salt solution such as Gatorade, which is available in a powder form to be reconstituted with water. If this is not available, one may make a "home brew" by mixing ¼ teaspoon table salt, 10 teaspoons table sugar, and 1 liter (approximately 1 quart) of water. An infant of one year of age requires 1 liter per day under normal conditions. This may double with fever and warm

weather conditions, and may be even higher if diarrhea is present.

The vast majority of illnesses in children are caused
by virus infections, including the common cold, most
throat infections, and most cases of diarrhea. In the
average uncomplicated case these can be managed by
symptomatic treatment. Antibiotics are indicated for
use in the treatment of specific diseases caused by bacteria infections such as ear infections, pneumonia,
and urinary tract infections.

Most upper respiratory infections are common
colds and last about 4 to 5 days. They are characterized by low grade fever, watery nasal secretions
which may or may not become thicker, and a mild
cough, often persisting late in the illness. Symptomatic treatment includes maintaining adequate
fluid intake, treatment of fever, and the giving of
decongestants, which are available without prescription. One should consult a physician if the fever is
greater than 39.5°C (103°F), the rate of breathing is
greater than 25 breaths per minute, or the breathing is
labored.

In most children, cough is a symptom of either
irritation to the back of the throat or the collection of
mucus and secretions in the nose. In general, this will
tend to be a dry, irritative type of cough, which is
more disturbing than a sign of serious illness. A deep
and moist cough, along with rapid and labored
breathing, should alert one to the possibility of
pneumonia or other lower respiratory disease and
should be evaluated by a physician. In addition, a
barking type of cough may occur in croup, a viral illness that affects the voice box or larynx and upper
windpipe. If the cough is accompanied by difficulty in
breathing or swallowing, drooling, or high fever, the
child should be seen by a physician.

Vomiting and Diarrhea

While vomiting and diarrhea usually represent a transient viral illness, gastroenteritis, this may be particularly troublesome and annoying for the care of children on a camping trip. Gastroenteritis or an intestinal virus is generally a self-limited disorder of 2 or 3 days duration. It must be distinguished from food poisoning and other more serious causes of "upset stomach" or stomachache.

Food poisoning occurs 2 to 6 hours following ingestion of contaminated food, affects a number of persons who shared the same food, and is not accompanied by fever. Appendicitis is characterized by low-grade fever, repeated vomiting, and pain initially felt throughout the abdomen which later becomes localized to the lower right section of the abdomen. If these symptoms are present or if there is pain upon hopping up and down, a sign of irritation to the lining of the abdomen, the child should be evaluated by a physician.

In general, gastroenteritis may be treated by a bland diet with the encouragement of liquids. If there is vomiting, this should include Coca-Cola which, when shaken to remove the carbonation, acts to settle the stomach. Other clear liquids that one may use include tea and noncitrus juices.

Small infants are more susceptible to dehydration due to their rapid fluid loss and small size. This may be prevented by the use of a powdered Gatorade solution or by the mixture described in an earlier section of the chapter. An infant of 1 year of age would require at least 1 quart of liquids for daily maintenance and, with the loss of water through diarrhea, at least an additional quart.

Most illnesses in children are self-limited and of short duration; these may be managed effectively by the simple measures outlined above. In general, common sense will be your guide, and these problems will not interfere with your vacation. One should err on the side of caution, however, in the case of small infants.

According to Mark and other doctors, the following should be part of your emergency kit:

Medications
*Antihistamines
*Adrenalin kit (if history of systemic allergic reaction to insect bite)
*Tetracycline (if backpacking in areas of exposure)
Antibacterial ointment
Calamine lotion
Aspirin or acetaminophen
Syrup of ipecac

Supplies
Gauze sponges, sterile
Ace bandage, 2" width
Nonadherent dressings
Cloth to fashion a sling

*Require Rx

24

The Solo Wilderness Traveler

Imagine yourself. Alone. During a solo cross-country hike across the canyon lands of Utah. Descending from the high route to the Colorado River. Scrambling along a limestone traverse twenty feet above the creekbed. A loaded pack constantly pulls you over backwards. You experience a crumbling foothold, and the sinking feeling of a fall you know cannot be good. Lying on your back in a shallow stream, you realize what has happened. When you try to rise, you realize you can't bend your left elbow.

What do you do now, 40 miles from the nearest help?

To tell us about solo wilderness travel, let me introduce you to an extraordinary outdoorsman, Ronald Meng, M.D. Ron approaches the outdoors as he approaches medicine, that is, with a 110% effort. Ron is a senior fellow in Cardiovascular and Thoracic Surgery at Rush-Presbyterian-St. Luke's Medical Center in Chicago, and an emergency medicine specialist. He is an expert mountaineer and backpacker and has climbed Mt. Cotopaxi (19,600 ft.) in Ecuador and Mt. Rainier (14,400 ft.) in Washington. He was, by the way, the medical officer on the Cotopaxi climb. He has backpacked across much of the Canadian and American Rockies and the Canyonlands of Utah. Although he makes most of his camps alone, perhaps we can join him for awhile and learn about the philosophy of caring for yourself when alone in the wilderness.

Ron defines survival as saving enough of oneself as a functional being for rehabilitation once the necessary measures are again at hand. The degree of rehabilitation required varies from simply rest and relaxation to life or limb-saving measures requiring hospitalization. Solo travel means total self-reliance, and injury significantly hampers one's ability to provide for warmth, food, and shelter in the already difficult circumstances imposed by solo wilderness travel. Thus, accidents or mistakes that lead to significant injury rapidly and dramatically escalate the situation from an adventure to struggle for survival.

Because of this, people have long thought solo wilderness travel to be crazy or foolhardy, but the mountain men of the West were not crazy, and the backpackers, ski mountaineers, and mountain climbers who find the sport exhilarating are not crazy. The beauty of relying solely on one's knowledge and skills in wilderness adventure can only be explained philosophically, but it must be appealing because it is gaining in popularity. Those who engage in this sport intentionally, however, are not the intended readers of this chapter. They know the risks involved in solo travel, and their mastery of the art of wilderness living and survival techniques allows them to take those risks and maintain a margin of safety.

Lest you decide not to read this chapter because you never go into the wilderness alone, let me assure you that *anyone* can be in a solo-survival situation. If during a group wilderness trip one person is injured, another stays with the injured person, and still another goes for help, a survival situation develops. Lost equipment, food shortage, and sudden inclement weather or other natural catastrophe can turn a holiday into a personal survival situation. In addition, anyone who travels through wilderness areas by snowmobile, car, or airplane is subject to a disaster that would dictate self-reliance. Thus, we can dispense right away with the cliché, "It can't happen to me."

What are the factors involved in solo wilderness survival? The stresses are the same as those our ancestors faced for survival. Nature makes the rules and demands that we flow with them, but nature also provides resources for living within them. The fundamental realization for you as a solo traveler must be that you are totally reliant upon yourself to maintain a thin margin of safety. This goes far to prepare you for any situation, since it dictates that all possible advantages to ensure safety be taken. You may be in top physical condition, but you must understand and respect your limitations. Conserve your strength and take no chances. Be expert in providing and maintaining the necessary equipment, including reserve and emergency equipment. Be expert in techniques of wilderness living, and know several ways to provide shelter and start fires, and how long each method takes. Be able to predict weather changes and to obtain water, and be sure you understand the implications of each terrain for efficient travel. Finally, you need the experience and common sense to make correct decisions regarding problems that develop.

Injuries sustained by a solo traveler demand observance of the same basic principles that apply to any wilderness injury. The initial response must be one of emotional stabilization, for the situation will require all the judgement and cool thinking that you can muster. Only with emotional stability can the necessary decisions be made and treatments carried out. Physical stabilization requires, of course, first aid, but medical care in wilderness situations often requires more than simple measures. Deeper knowledge is necessary to provide detailed and specific professional treatment and prevention of possible complications.

Because of the hardships involved with caring for yourself and using your own resources, certain additional principles become important. As a solo traveler, you must apply all the necessary medical care to yourself. Furthermore, you must retain the ability to survive wilderness challenges and obtain help. Extensive knowledge and capability, unfailing willpower, and considerable ingenuity are required for the victim to function as both doctor and messenger.

The ability to survive the stress wilderness situations varies directly with how well survival techniques have been ingrained into instinct. Survival skills can enable you to surmount fear, decreased capabilities due to injury, and the stresses of the environment. Their proper application can make the difference between a fatality and merely a cold, wet, and hungry night.

Prevention of Survival Situations

The goal of any solo traveler should be complete prevention of any situation that compromises security. Concentrate on this to the utmost, because the consequences are far more serious for a solo traveler than for group travelers. Nowhere is the adage, "An ounce of prevention is worth a pound of cure," more appropriate.

The first rule for prevention of survival situations is *extensive and detailed communication of your itinerary to* others, so that if you are injured or become lost, rescuers can be efficiently dispatched. It is even better if the trail is marked for rescuers to follow.

Appropriate equipment is very important, since equipment forms the nucleus of the resources available in a wilderness setting. Your equipment must be chosen with attention to reliability, versatility, and weight to enable you to handle any situation that might develop.

Wilderness living technique that maintains the body's vital functions and homeostasis (internal balance) plays an important role in preventing danger. High-altitude climbing provides an excellent example. Dangers include the cold, dry atmosphere, which is poor in oxygen and transparent to ultraviolet irradiation. Failure to acclimatize slowly to high altitude could cause high-altitude sickness, pulmonary edema, or cerebral edema. The wind and increased ultraviolet irradiation can cause sun and windburn and snow blindness. At high altitude, excess body water is lost because of the increase in breathing and sweating; thirst somehow fails as a strong drive, and obtaining water is difficult. Failure to drink enough water to keep the urine color very pale leads to progressive dehydration. Proper clothing is required to prevent frostbite. Poor nutrition and water intake, inadequate clothing, and inadequate shelter at high altitude all increase the risk of hypothermia, the biggest killer of expedition members. Although sleep is difficult, adequate rest and recuperation are required each day. Even care of the feet is important, since blisters and ingrown toenails can effectively immobilize the solo traveler. Any lapse in protection against these dangers could be fatal. These are some of the principles of bivouac camping, a euphemism for wilderness living by survival techniques. Bivouac camping can be comfortable and sometimes even luxurious, but it is based on stoicism. There is some risk, to be sure, and occasionally severe discomfort, but pushing oneself to the limit usually defines new limits. The well-conditioned body is elastic, capable of many things and limited only by the mind.

Obviously, then, good general health is required for anyone planning an outdoor adventure. Chronic medical conditions unacceptably increase the risks. Good physical conditioning not only makes planned travel much easier and more enjoyable, but, is absolutely indispensable in survival situations. The most important physical attribute for this application is endurance, which is best obtained by aerobic conditioning. This cardiovascular fitness is manifested by the ability to maintain prolonged increased heart work for adequate blood supply to exercising tissues. Agility is also important to the wilderness traveler and is manifested by flexibility, balance, and quickness. Proper immunizations include anti-tetanus shots and any others recommended specifically for the area to be visited.

The most important preventive measure is *mental conditioning*. The only reasonable rule anywhere is not to take unnecessary chances, and always weigh the possible loss against the possible gain. A solidly ingrained realization that accidents cannot be afforded lessens the probability of a crippling mishap. Therefore, it must be accepted that regardless of preparation and capabilities, there are still limitations that must be respected. Reasonable goals for distance traveled, altitude gained, and length of work day must be set and adhered to, and equipment and rations planned accordingly. It must also be accepted that any development that reduces the full capability of the solo traveler enhances the risk in a survival situation. Lost equipment, situations that require unavailable equipment, or signs of illness, including chest or abdominal pains, fainting, vomiting or diarrhea, fever, chills, or other signs of infection, all enhance the risks and, therefore, dictate evacuation. Usually, these problems develop slowly enough to allow sufficient time for orderly retreat before the situation becomes an emergency one. Even a slight injury should prompt consideration of evacuation because it increases the risk of a second injury. The seriousness of the predicament increases greatly with each subsequent accident.

Just surviving routine conditions encountered in solo travel situations is very difficult, so setbacks caused by accidents or mistakes are intolerable. As wide a safety margin as possible must be maintained by application of preventive measures and aggressive, logical treatment of any development that tends to narrow or eliminate the safety margin.

Coping with Survival Situations

Emotional Stability

The first requirement for successfully handling an emergency when alone is to *regain composure*. The ability to analyze a problem rationally and then select and pursue a direct, logical course toward a solution is common sense, but it may be difficult to muster in the presence of a survival challenge.

The reaction to fear is the determinant. Fear of the unknown or of discomfort is a universal, natural response. In combination with pain, loneliness, boredom, hunger, and tiredness, it fuels a vicious cycle that escalates rapidly to frank panic, with hasty, poorly-thought-out decisions and rash, foolhardy, and dangerous actions. Panic saps energy and erodes the will to survive. It leads to fatigue, the embodiment of lost confidence and lost hope. It is an apathetic escape that is irreversible. Once this stage is reached, all is lost. It must, therefore, be prevented at all costs.

The novice is easy prey to fear. For a novice in the wilderness, outcome often depends more on attitude than the nature of the emergency. Escalation of a minor accident to an emergency often results solely because panic prevented initiation of proper survival techniques.

Fear can be conquered with self-confidence. Be assured that, regardless of your situation, others have been through the same thing and survived. Regardless of your location, others have been there before intentionally and lived by adjusting to the demands. Forget about being a comfort-loving animal who must be rested, fed, and transported luxuriously. Your body can take more than you think. It is limited only by your mind.

The will to survive is a very powerful force indeed. With this attitude, performance does not suffer, no matter what the insult, because something can always be done to improve the situation. Pain, loneliness, and boredom can be overcome with direction of purpose and activity. Self-distraction by talking aloud or singing is helpful. Knowledge that one can survive for weeks without food lessens hunger, and after two or three days of fasting, hunger ceases to be a problem. When food is again available, it becomes a treat, a reward for a job well done. Finally, tiredness can be overcome by sleep. Sleep passes time that might otherwise be spent worrying, and it strengthens the body and the mind, providing confidence through a new outlook on awakening. Thinking of the job ahead as many small jobs makes the whole situation seem less awesome and restores initiative. With these attitudes and application of competent technical and physical skills to available resources, the battle is half won. Imagination, ingenuity, and a good sense of humor will usually illuminate a clear route to success.

Physical Stability

Steps taken immediately after injury vary according to specific situations. In all but the life-threatening conditions of massive bleeding or major neck or chest trauma, the first priority is reaching safety. Get out of the water, away from the avalanche, cliff, or rock fall. Gain protection from animals or lightning, and if climbing, belay solidly. Only in a secure position can first aid proceed. After specific first-aid measures have been performed, assess your entire body. Not uncommonly, to the surprise of the victim, other injuries will be found that had previously been overshadowed by the pain or drama of the catastrophe. The newly found injuries must then be treated, and at this time steps must be taken to prevent complications such as shock. Record keeping should begin formally at this point.

Clearly, most minor injuries can be just as well self-treated as treated by another. These include minor lacerations and burns. However, major injuries that threaten life either directly or indirectly by creating major disability are another matter. Severe sprains, dislocations and, of course, fractures are extremely disabling and difficult to overcome. The solo traveler learns always to suspect a fracture with bone and joint injuries and to act accordingly and take no chances. Sprains require only external support by wrapping with any flexible material at hand and stoic denial of pain. Dislocations and fractures must be reduced and splinted from the joint above to the joint below by any material available. It is beneficial to reduce swelling by cooling with water, snow, or even sand or rocks. Excessively tight bandages must be avoided to prevent swelling and blockage of blood flow to the extremity. Compound fractures must be cleansed and dressed as well as splinted.

Another special situation is loss of consciousness. Once consciousness is regained, stabilization must be carried out quickly because unconsciousness may return. The climber who regains consciousness after a fall must first belay solidly in a protected position to prevent falling further or being hit by falling rocks. Self-treatment of all injuries and evacuation must proceed efficiently in the most secure fashion. Speed and accuracy after regaining consciousness can mean the difference between life and death.

Any laceration causing severe bleeding is also a serious threat. This is perhaps the only indication for tourniquet use left in trauma medicine. Although most bleeding can be controlled by direct pressure, if the isolated victim loses consciousness or weakens, too much blood could be lost for survival. Thus, a tourniquet in these situations could be lifesaving, but remember that it places the extremity at great risk.

Each of these conditions has in common the development of a very dangerous complication: shock. In addition to psychological shock after severe injury, the body is at risk for low pulse, low blood pressure, or circulatory collapse. This risk is present regardless of the type of injury and must be routinely expected and vigorously prevented. The immobilization and incapacitation that can result are disastrous for the totally self-dependent solo traveler. Prevention consists of absolute rest, frequent sips of liquid to prevent dehydration, and maintenance of body heat by clothing, shelter, and food.

Evacuation

After optimum stabilization, the problem becomes one of obtaining help. Whether this is done by immediate self-evacuation or by remaining in a reasonable, well-controlled situation depends upon factors such as physical capabilities and environment. The best way to decide is to formally categorize and judge the relative advantages and disadvantages of each factor in the given situation. Whichever method is preferred, however, basic wilderness living technique is required.

Body homeostasis (internal balance) depends most urgently on minimizing harsh exposure, since exposure can kill far more quickly than thirst or starvation. In high-altitude situations, with inherently low oxygen availability, descent is mandatory to maximize oxygen for exercising and healing tissues. The proper balance between heat loss and heat production must be maintained by proper utilization of shelter, fire, clothes, and food. Weather dictates the degree of protection from the environment required. Water balance must be maintained by adequate water intake and prevention of excessive water loss. Finally, various methods of signaling for help must be available for use at a moment's notice. These techniques are liberally covered in survival books and are not the focus of this chapter, but they cannot be disassociated from the situation created by injury of the solo wilderness traveler.

The general recommendation for getting help in a survival situation is to remain stationary because rest maximizes energy conservation and recovery. In the special case of the solo wilderness traveler, however, this is risky because the length of time that the traveler can support himself or herself may be very brief. Thus, only in specific circumstances is this the best course of action. If you are lost, if the location of help is unknown, if you are unable to navigate or unable to travel, then clearly you should remain where you are. If you have an ideal campsite or are stranded with a vehicle, and especially if the weather is poor, this approach becomes even more attractive. Place your confidence in your ability to signal effectively and in the knowledge that others will search for you because of the itinerary you provided.

In most other situations, you are better advised to travel as efficiently as possible towards help. Certainly it is necessary if your present location is unacceptable because of exposure, lack of water, or the possibility of avalanche, lightning, or flash flood. In this case, you might travel only far enough to avoid immediate danger and then wait. Usually, however, continued movement towards help is the best policy as long as appropriate precautions are taken.

Generally these precautions are simply the rules of preventing survival situations. First, leave abundant information regarding your direction of travel and physical condition. Leave written notes or triplicate trail markers. Second, carry the necessary gear, but nothing extra. Third, minimize energy expenditure by keeping a steady, comfortable pace, taking frequent, short tests, and generally following the path of least resistance within a reasonably straight line. Fourth, always be ready to signal effectively at a moment's notice. Finally, conserve body homeostasis by the use of all survival skills available.

If you know where you are, you probably know the best place to go for help. Either you know the area, or you have a map and compass. If you don't know where you are or where to go, there are still ways of finding help. Survival books describe techniques for trailblazing and navigation based on natural phenomena and "ded" (deduced) reckoning.

Travel is not impossible even in the face of what would appear to be a severe disability. One solo climber descended 8,000 feet to safety after breaking his leg, by using his ice axe as a crutch. Another descended a peak with frozen toes, knowing that if he first thawed them and then descended, there would be more pain and greater risk of damage and infection.

The situation described at the beginning of this chapter is not imagined or contrived. It actually happened. To me. And it required knowledge and application of the principles of solo survival.

I knew my elbow was dislocated, because when I tried to get out of the stream, it actually bent backwards in what we call a posterior dislocation. I knew that there might be an associated fracture, and I knew that the artery to my hand might be blocked. I immediately assessed my surroundings. True, I was in a stream, but in no danger of drowning, being washed over a waterfall, or covered by a rock fall, so I remained where I was. Next, I made sure that there were no other injuries. There was no pulse in my wrist, so immediate reduction of the dislocation was not only desirable but necessary. Knowing that traction and countertraction and gentle manipulation of the elbow are necessary for safe and successful reduction, I improvised a system to provide these essentials. By tying a rope around my left wrist, passing it around the log next to me, and tying the other end to my chest harness, I created a system whereby when I leaned back I could provide traction of my forearm away from my shoulder, stretching the elbow joint. With this method my right hand was free to help guide my left elbow back into position. "Hold your breath, count to three, and lean back," I said to myself. The elbow slid into position, with only mild worsening of the pain. I was happy to feel a pulse in my left wrist once again, and I bent my arm across my chest and held it in position there with a sling made from the rope.

After a difficult climb out of the ravine, I pulled my

gear up after me and settled down for the night. Cool compresses throughout the night kept the swelling down and eased the pain. The next day I fashioned a more secure sling, cached the gear that I wouldn't need and couldn't carry anyway, and simply began walking toward a ranch I found on the map. Two days later I met two cowboys, who not only took me to a hospital but also recovered my cached gear. All in all it was a trying situation, but rewarding in that I was able to salvage myself in what could have been an extremely dangerous predicament. My arm is essentially normal, and the experience has strengthened my confidence and, I might add, my respect for the wilderness.

25

The Emergency Kit

Knowing what to do when a medical emergency occurs outdoors is the most important thing for the person involved. Almost as important as knowing what to do is having what you need to carry out emergency medical care. I have hunted and fished with an awful lot of people who were caught unprepared for problems and swore that next trip they were *definitely* going to have an emergency kit. Well, usually, the next trip they again had no kit or they had purchased or made up the most inexpensive kit available, usually consisting of a box of Bandaids and a few aspirin. After spending thousands of dollars for a trip, equipment and other supplies they skimp on the things they need to care for themselves. If an electronic fish finder or a rifle is worth spending hundreds of dollars on, how much is your own health worth? You would not go hunting without ammo; you would not go fishing without your tackle box; you would not go camping without your tent; and you should not go anywhere without an emergency kit and the knowledge needed to use it. Let me run down the list of commonly recommended items for the kit, their uses, and amount required of each. Remember, you don't need a ten-year supply of each thing in your kit—just enough for emergencies. As things are used up, replace them. This serves to cut down on bulk and forces you to inventory your kit and keep things up to date.

Contents

First you should have a waterproof container filled with all medications you normally take as prescribed by your family doctor. Have enough of them to last the entire trip and some extra—just in case. Each medicine should be labeled so that someone else can find and identify it if you are not able to.

Second, if you are an asthmatic, have a history of severe allergies, or are allergic to insect stings, you should obtain, by prescription from a doctor, an insect sting kit. Not having one could cost you your life.

Third, also from your doctor, you should have a prescription antibiotic which is safe for you to use, a jar of Silvadene burn ointment and some strong pain pills, Empirin #3 or Tylenol #3, if you are not allergic to them.

Now let's talk about the things you can simply go to your neighborhood drug store and get yourself.

Amount

1	Thermometer in a rigid case—to measure body temperature, fever, or water temperature for treatment of frostbite.
1	Plastic squeeze bottle of balanced salt solution—to irrigate foreign bodies or irritants from eyes.
4	2-tablet foil or plastic pack aspirin or Tylenol packets—for headache, fever, or pain relief.
4	Safety pins—to make a sling or hold bandages in place and to relieve blood blisters under nails.
2	Rubber bands—to use as tourniquets between heart and bite for poison insect and snake bites.

1	3-foot square cloth—to use as sling or bandage with safety pins.
4	2-tablet packets or blister pack of allergy tablets such as Chlor-Trimenton 4 mg.—for allergy or hay fever.
2	Foil packets of germicide solution such as Betadine solution—for soaking burns and cuts.
2	Foil packets of scrub soap such as Betadine scrub—for washing cuts, abrasions and any broken skin.
1	Heavy drainage pack with 12 x 18 sterile pad for covering large wounds and padding fractures and sprains.
1	Long gauge bandage roll such as Kerlix 5-yard roll—for wrapping and covering large cuts of head, extremities or trunk.
1	Set sterile tweezers and scissors—for removal of splinters and cutting bandages and clothing.
2	Sterile eye pads—to cover eyes and also as cotton wadding to use in ear injuries.
2	Antiseptic towelettes—to clean minor scrapes and scratches.
1	Roll of tape—to hold dressings in place.
2	Sterile wooden tongue depressors—for application of ointments and as splints.
3	Packets of ointment such as Acu Dyne or Betadine ointment—for use on burns and cuts and punctures.

12	Adhesive strips such as Bandaids — small cut coverage.
2	Packets of cotton tipped applicators — for removal of foreign bodies from corner of eye, or from sclera (white of eye) and multi-purpose.
1	Small plastic bottle of syrup of ipecac — to induce vomiting after poisoning.
1	Small container of pain relieving anti-septic such as Camphophenic — to relieve pain of fever blisters and sores in mouth.
1	Small container oil of cloves — to relieve pain of fractured or decayed teeth.
1	Packet of Steri Strip skin tapes — to close small clean cuts on skin.
1	4" elastic bandage or Ace wrap — to support sprains of wrist, elbow, knee or ankle — also for use as pressure bandage.
1	Sterile straight edge razor blade — to incise prior to suction over venomous bites.

This kit is relatively inexpensive and has virtually everything you need to care for injuries until medical aid can be reached. Knowing what to have won't do you any good unless you have it. Don't be one of those caught unprepared outdoors. I hope that this book will be a help to you, and that it will add to your health, self confidence, and enjoyment of the wild places we all love so much.

This partial listing is taken from the National Clearinghouse for Poison Control Centers Bulletin, Volume 23, No. 8, August 1979, Directory of Poison Control Centers.

These locations and telephone numbers are correct as of August, 1979. Since changes occur frequently, verify the location of the particular poison center closest to your destination before you depart.

Directory of Poison Control Centers

Alabama

ANNISTON
205 237-5421
Ext. 307

N.E. Alabama Regional Medical
  Center
400 E. 10th St. 36201

MOBILE
205 473-3325

University of So. Alabama Medical
  Center
400 E. 10th St. 36201

Alaska

ANCHORAGE
907 274-6535

Providence Hospital
3200 Providence Drive 99504

Arizona

FLAGSTAFF
602 774-5233
Ext. 255

Flagstaff Hospital
1215 N. Beaver St. 86001

TUCSON
602 626-6016

Arizona Health Services Center
University of Arizona 85721

Arkansas

LITTLE ROCK
501 661-6161   University of Arkansas Medical
                               Center
                               4301 W. Markham St. 72201

California

ORANGE
714 634-5988   University of California
                               Irvine Medical Center
                               101 City Drive South 92668

SAN FRANCISCO
800 792-0720   San Francisco Bay Area Poison
                               Center

Canal Zone

BALBOA HEIGHTS
52-7500   Gorgas Hospital
                               Box 0

Colorado

DENVER
303 629-1123   Rocky Mt. Poison Center
                               West 8th & Cherokee 80204

Connecticut

NEW HAVEN
203 436-1960   Drug Information Center
                               Dept. of Pharm. Serv.
                               Yale-New Haven Hospital
                               789 Howard Ave. 06504

Delaware

WILMINGTON
302 655-3389   Poison Information Service
                               501 W. 14th St. 19899

District of Columbia

WASHINGTON, DC
202 745-2000   Children's Hospital National
                      Medical Center
                      111 Michigan Avenue, N.W. 20010

Florida

MIAMI
305 325-6799   Jackson Memorial Hospital
                      Att: Pharmacy
                      1611 N.W. 12th Ave. 33136

TALLAHASSEE
904 599-5411   Tallahassee Mem. Reg. Medical
                      Center
                      Magnolia Drive and Miccouskee
                      Road 32304

Georgia

ATLANTA
404 588-4400   Georgia Poison Control Center
800 282-5846   Grady Memorial Hospital
  (Toll Free)   80 Butler Street, S.E. 30303
404 525-3323
  (Deaf)
SAVANNAH
912 355-5228   Savannah Regional Poison Center
                      Department of Emergency Med.
                      Memorial Medical Center
                      P.O. Box 23089 31403⁻

Guam

AGANA
344-9265   Pharmacy Service, Box 7696
344-9354   U.S. Naval Regional Medical
                          Center (GUAM)
                      FPO San Francisco, CA 96630

Hawaii

HONOLULU
808 941-4411   Kapiolani-Children's Medical
                            Center
                            1319 Punahou Street 96826

Idaho

TOLL-FREE-STATEWIDE NUMBER 1-800 632-8000

BOISE
208 376-1211   St. Alphonsus Hospital
Ext. 707   1055 N. Curtis Road 83704

Illinois

CHICAGO
312 942-5969   Rush-Presbyterian-St. Luke's
                           Medical Center
                           1753 West Congress Parkway
                           60612

SPRINGFIELD
217 753-3330   Central and Southern Poison
1-800 252-2022   Resource Center
                           St. John's Hospital
                           800 East Carpenter 62702

Indiana

INDIANAPOLIS
317 630-7351   Wishard Memorial Hospital
800 382-9097   1001 West 10th Street 46202
  (TOLL-FREE)
SOUTH BEND
219 234-2151   St. Joseph's Hospital
Ext. 253, 264   811 East Madison Street 46622

Iowa

IOWA CITY
319 356-2922
800 272-6477
(All Iowa
Residents)

University of Iowa Hospital and
Clinics
Pharmacy Department 52240

Kansas

KANSAS CITY
913 588-6633

University of Kansas Medical
Center
39th and Rainbow Boulevard 66103

WICHITA
316 685-2151
Ext. 7515

Wesley Medical Center
550 North Hillside Avenue 67214

Kentucky

LEXINGTON
606 233-5320

Drug Information Center
University of Kentucky Medical
Center
40536

LOUISVILLE
502 589-8222

Norton-Children's Hospital
Pharmacy Department
200 East Chestnut Street 40202

PRESTONSBURG
606 886-8511

Poison Control Center
Highlands Regional Medical
Center
41653

Louisiana

MONROE
318 342-3008

Northeast University
Department of Pharmacology
Drug Information Center
700 University Avenue 70201

SHREVEPORT
318 425-1524   LSU Medical Center
                            P.O. Box 33932 71130

Maine

STATE COORDINATOR
1-800 442-6305   Maine Poison Control Center
                            Portland 04102

PORTLAND
207 871-2950   Maine Medical Center
1-800 442-6305   22 Bramhall Street 04102
(TOLL FREE)

Maryland

STATE COORDINATOR
301 528-7604   Maryland Poison Information
                               Center
                            University of Maryland School of
                               Pharmacy
                            21201

BALTIMORE
301 528-7701   Maryland Poison Information
800 492-2414   Center
(TOLL FREE   University of Maryland School of
IN MARYLAND)   Pharmacy
                            636 W. Lombard Street 21201

Massachusetts

BOSTON
617 232-2120   Massachusetts Poison Control
1-800 682-9211   System
                            30 Longwood Avenue 02115

Michigan

DETROIT
313 494-5711   Children's Hospital of Michigan
                            3901 Beaubien 48201

GRAND RAPIDS
800 442-4571   Western Michigan Poison Center
  800 632-2727   1840 Wealthy, S.E. 49506
  (TOLL FREE)
MARQUETTE
800 562-9723   Marquette General Hospital
                      420 West Magnetic Drive 49855

Minnesota

MINNEAPOLIS
612 588-0616   North Memorial Hospital
                      3220 Lowry North 55422

ROCHESTER
507 285-5123   Southeastern Minnesota Poison
                          Control Center
                      St. Mary's Hospital
                      1216 Second Street, S.W. 55901

Mississippi

BILOXI
601 377-2516   USAF Hospital Keesler
  377-6555   Keesler Air Force Base
  377-6556   39534

UNIVERSITY
601 234-1522   School of Pharmacy
                      University of Mississippi 38677

Missouri

STATE COORDINATOR
314 751-2713   Missouri Division of Health
                      Jefferson City 65102

COLUMBIA
314 882-4141   University of Missouri Medical
                          Center
                      807 Stadium Road 65201

SPRINGFIELD
417 831-9746   Lester E. Cox Medical Center
1-800 492-4824   1423 North Jefferson Street 65802
(TOLL FREE)

Montana

STATE COORDINATOR

1-800 525-5042	Department of Health and Environmental Sciences Helena 59601
1-800 525-5042	Montana Poison Control System

Nebraska

OMAHA

402 553-5400 800 642-9999 (NEBRASKA) 800 228-9515 (SURROUNDING STATES)	Children's Memorial Hospital 44th and Dewey Streets 68105

Nevada

LAS VEGAS

702 385-1277	Southern Nevada Memorial Hospital 1800 West Charleston Boulevard 89102

RENO

702 323-2041	St. Mary's Hospital 235 West 6th 89503

New Hampshire

HANOVER

603 643-4000	New Hampshire Poison Center Mary Hitchcock Hospital 2 Maynard Street 03755

New Jersey

ATLANTIC CITY

609 344-4081	Atlantic City Medical Center 1925 Pacific Avenue 08401

NEPTUNE
800 822-9761

Jersey Shore Medical Center-Fitkin
    Hospital
1945 Corlies Avenue 07753

NEWARK
201 926-7240
   926-7241, 2,
   926-7243

Newark Beth Israel Medical Center
201 Lyons Avenue 07112

New Mexico

STATE COORDINATOR
505 843-2551

The University of New Mexico
    Albuquerque 87131

STATE COORDINATOR
ALBUQUERQUE
505 843-2551
(1-800 432-6866
Within NM)

New Mexico Poison, Drug Inf. &
    Med. Crisis Center
University of New Mexico 87131

New York

BUFFALO
716 878-7654

Western New York Poison Control
    Center at Children's Hospital
219 Bryant Street 14222

NYACK
914 358-5581
   358-6200
Ext. 451, 452

Hudson Valley Poison Center
Nyack Hospital (Pharmacy)
North Midland Avenue 10960

SYRACUSE
315 476-7529

Onondaga County Health
    Department
Poison Control Center
Upstate Medical Center
750 East Adams Street 13210

North Carolina

DURHAM
919 684-8111

Duke University Medical Center
Box 3007 27710

North Dakota

BISMARCK
701 223-4357   Bismarck Hospital
                                300 North 7th Street 58501

FARGO
701 280-5575   St. Luke's Hospital
                                Fifth Street at Mills Avenue 58102

Ohio

CINCINNATI
513 872-5111   Drug and Poison Information
                                    Center
                                University of Cincinnati Medical
                                    Center
                                Room 7701, Bridge 45267

CLEVELAND
216 231-4455   Academy of Medicine
                                11001 Cedar Avenue 44106

YOUNGSTOWN
216 746-2222   Mahoning Valley Poison Center
                                St. Elizabeth Hospital and Medical
                                    Center
                                1044 Belmont Avenue 44505

ZANESVILLE
614 454-4221   Bethesda Hospital
                                Poison Information Center
                                2951 Maple Avenue 43701

Oklahoma

STATE COORDINATOR
405 271-5454   Oklahoma Poison Control Center
        or   Oklahoma Children's Memorial
800 522-4611   Hospital
                                P.O. Box 26307 73126

OKLAHOMA CITY
405 271-5454   Oklahoma Poison Control Center
        or   Oklahoma Children's Memorial
800 522-4611   Hospital
(Oklahoma)   P.O. Box 26307 73126

Oregon

PORTLAND
503 225-8500

Oregon Poison Control and Drug
    Information Center
University of Oregon Health
    Sciences Center
3181 S.W. Sam Jackson
Park Road 97201

Pennsylvania

DANVILLE
717 275-6116

Susquehanna Poison Center
Geisinger Medical Center
North Academy Avenue 17821

ERIE
814 452-3232

Northwest Poison Center
St. Vincent Health Center
P.O. Box 740 16512

PHILADELPHIA
215 922-5523
    922-5524

Philadelphia Poison Information
321 University Avenue 19104

Puerto Rico

STATE COORDINATOR
809 765-4880
    765-0615

University of Puerto Rico
Rio Piedras

RIO PIEDRAS
809 764-3515

Medical Center of Puerto Rico
    00936

Rhode Island

KINGSTON
401 792-2775
    792-2762

College of Pharmacy
University of Rhode Island 02881

South Carolina

CHARLESTON
803 792-4201

Poison Information Service
Medical University of South
    Carolina
171 Ashley Avenue 29403

COLUMBIA
803 765-7359

Poison and Drug Information
Center
College of Pharmacy
Room 313 Coker Life Science Bldg.
University of S.C. 29208

South Dakota

RAPID CITY
605 343-3333
1-800 742-8925
(TOLL FREE)

West River Poison Center
Rapid City Regional Hospital East
57701

SIOUX FALLS
605 336-3894
1-800 952-0123
(TOLL FREE)

McKennan Hospital Poison Center
800 East 21st Street 57101

Tennessee

MEMPHIS
901 528-6048

University of Tennessee
College of Pharmacy
874 Union Avenue 38163

NASHVILLE
615 322-3391

Vanderbilt University Hospital
21st and Garland 37232

Texas

GALVESTON
713 765-1420
or
713 765-1561

Southeast Texas Poison Control
Center
8th and Mechanic Streets 77550

LUBBOCK
806 792-1011
Ext. 315

Methodist Hospital Pharmacy
3615 19th Street 79410

SAN ANTONIO
512 223-1481

Texas County Hospital District
c/o Department of Pediatrics
University of Texas Medical School
at San Antonio
7703 Floyd Drive 78229

WICHITA FALLS
817 322-6771   Wichita General Hospital
                            Emergency Room
                            1600 8th Street 76301

Utah

SALT LAKE CITY
801 581-2151   Intermountain Regional Poison
                            Control Center
                            50 North Medical Drive 84132

Virginia

CHARLOTTESVILLE
804 924-5543   Blue Ridge Poison Center
                            University of Virginia Hospital
                            22908

RICHMOND
804 786-9123   Virginia Poison Center
                            Virginia Commonwealth
                            University
                            Box 763 MCV Station 23298

Virgin Islands

ST. CROIX
809 773-1212   Charles Harwood Memorial
    773-1311   Hospital
Ext. 221   Christiansted 00820

ST. THOMAS
809 774-1321   Knud-Hansen Memorial Hospital
Ext. 224, 225   00801

Washington

BELLINGHAM
206 676-8400   St. Luke's General Hospital
    676-8401   809 East Chestnut Street 98225
1-800 562-8816
    562-8817
(TOLL FREE)

SEATTLE
206 634-5252   Children's Orthopedic Hospital
                           and Medical Center
                           4800 Sandpoint Way, N.E. 98105

YAKIMA
509 248-4400   Yakima Valley Memorial Hospital
                           2811 Tieton Drive 98902

West Virginia

CHARLESTON
304 348-4211   Charleston Area Medical Center
                           Memorial Division
                           3200 Noyes Avenue 25304

MORGANTOWN
304 293-5341   Mountain State Poison Center
                           Department of Pediatrics
                           West Virginia University Medical
                           Center 26506

Wisconsin

MADISON
608 262-3702   University Hospitals and Clinics
                           600 Highland Avenue 53792

MILWAUKEE
414 931-1010   Milwaukee Children's Hospital
                           1700 West Wisconsin 53233

Wyoming

STATE COORDINATOR
307 777-7955   Department of Health and Social
                           Services
                           Cheyenne 82001

CHEYENNE
307 635-9256   Wyoming Poison Center
                           DePaul Hospital
                           2600 East 18th Street 82001

Index